TOM TANCREDO

HATING AMERICA

TOM TANCREDO

HATING AMERICA

HATING AMERICA:
The Left's Long History Of Despising (And Slowly Destroying) Our Great Country

Former Congressman
TOM TANCREDO

With

PHIL ROSS

HATING AMERICA

TOM TANCREDO

HATING AMERICA

FIRST EDITION

Library of Congress Cataloging-in-Publication Data has been applied for.

ISBN 13:9781484968604

ISBN 10: 1484968603

For All Truly Patriotic Americans

Who Cherish Our Beloved Country

And Recoil At Political Correctness

HATING AMERICA

TABLE OF CONTENTS

HATING AMERICA

PROLOGUE

Winston Churchill, as usually was the case, was as spot-on as a spot of soothing English tea, when he said, "Socialism is a philosophy of failure, the creed of ignorance, and the gospel of envy, its inherent virtue is the equal sharing of misery."

Ignorance is a key word in that passage, and illiteracy is a good companion. Take the ill-advised protesters of the "Occupy" movement who commandeered Lower Manhattan's small Zuccotti Park for days on end in the fall of 2011 to ostensibly protest Wall Street's excesses, then saw their unwashed hordes grow in similar instances of civil disobedience in other cities, including outside the White House in January 2012, then in protest to the G8 meetings in Chicago in spring 2012. These cretins are emblematic of the mindset, or lack thereof, of today's leftists, whether they are tax-and-spend, socialistic liberals who form the base of the Democrat Party or hard-line Marxists who want to dismantle all of the cherished institutions that have made our country truly exceptional for more than 230 years. At every turn, these radicals desire – and unfortunately often succeed – to revise our history to suit their own selfish and collective (double meaning here) needs. The November 2012 re-election of Barack Obama unfortunately portends a further decline into the steep abyss of statism.

As "progressives," as they like to call themselves, "progress," they constantly hunger for increasing power to control all our lives, starting whenever they can with pre-school children and indoctrinating them with the socialist agenda, which, point-by-point, is counter to the shining principles on which our Founders laid a foundation. And these radicals accomplish their dastardly deeds in as shrill a manner as possible. When left-wingers cannot win an argument on logic and merit – of which they possess neither – they resort to yelling, screaming and name-calling. They comprise America's most virulent hate group; they despise the country we love and revel in tearing down all our cherished institutions. Witness the 2012 presidential campaign and the seemingly endless negativism that prevailed.

But back to the issue of illiteracy, which assumes other forms than the mere, literal meaning. No, there are such things as economic and civic illiteracy, and protesters like those in the Occupy movement have gone a long way in demonstrating they have been afflicted with both figurative applications. There is a deeper subset to the entire movement, however, and the evidence becomes more readily apparent as one delves into it with microscopic precision.

When Obama was elected to a second four-year term – despite 23 million unemployed Americans and a federal debt beyond $16 trillion -- it was painfully obvious that economic and civic illiteracy have transcended the unwashed Occupy Wall Street (OWS) masses and shockingly afflicted the general populace as well.

When asked simple questions as to "what" and "why" they were protesting, the OWS groupies could not, to a person, produce a coherent response, or if they did, it was a vague platitude about greedy capitalist-this or big, bad banker-that. It was clear to me, early on, that we were dealing with not only economic illiterates but civic illiterates as well. In the keynote speech to the Tea Party national convention in 2009, I had emphasized how Barack Obama was elected in 2008 because we do not have a civics/literacy test to vote. People who could not even spell the word "vote," or say it aloud in English, put a committed socialist ideologue in the White House, I reminded the Tea Partyers.

Couple all this with the Lamestream Media's typical coddling of the miscreants who populate the Occupy movement and you can see an uncanny like-mindedness, as my fellow conservative pundit, economist Walter Williams, put it. Williams wrote, a couple of months prior to the onset of OWS, that there exists a "gross media ignorance" about the Founders. Citing a backward, and incorrect, portrayal of the Founders' intent on positioning of the slavery issue by liberal *Time* magazine editor Richard Stengel, Williams, a black, argued that, if he did not know better, he would suspect a media conspiracy. "If I believed in conspiracies, I'd say Stengel's article is part of a leftist agenda to undermine respect for the founding values of our nation," professor Williams wrote. Trouble is, the Stengel episode seems to be the rule, not the exception, for those who falsely fashion themselves as objective when they are nothing more than cheerleaders for the Left and garden-variety radicals interested only in power.

The OWS phenomenon was not spontaneous and, as I said, it was well-orchestrated from the outset, despite ongoing denials by its participants and supporters, including President Obama, Vice President Joe Biden and such top-ranking Democrats as two of my former U.S. House colleagues, Minority Leader and former Speaker Nancy Pelosi and Debbie Wasserman Schultz, chair of the Democratic National Committee. Moreover, it also became increasingly clear that labor unions, especially those representing taxpayer-funded public employees, were ensuring the longevity of the protests and that plenty of succor from all the George Soros-connected radical front groups was keeping the pot sweet.

It gets even worse, though. Consider all of the following assortment of occurrences associated with the Fleabaggers, or (as at least one wag dubbed them) the Flea Party, not to be confused with the Tea Party, in manners, mien or basic hygiene:

-- After expressing support for the protesters, another former colleague, Chicago Democrat Rep. Jesse Jackson, Jr., son of the infamous left-wing political activist and shakedown artist, went public with a beyond-incredible plea -- an $804 billion "jobs" bill he was sponsoring. The younger Jackson, who is wrestling with new ethical, legal and health problems of his own making and resigned his seat, called on government to hire ALL unemployed Americans (all 14 million-plus, I presume) – for $40,000 each! Another sign of blatant economic illiteracy on the left.

-- Aaron Klein, a bright, young pundit and investigative reporter for *WND.com*, for which I also write a regular commentary column, produced strong evidence that, rather than a "spontaneous uprising," as the mainstream media maintained, the OWS crowds were meticulously organized with the Soros-linked millions. A public relations firm with a history of strategizing for Soros himself, Moveon.org and "a litany of anti-war groups" represented a march of Occupy protesters past millionaires' Manhattan homes, Klein disclosed. Because the firm's founder is tied to Obama and other Saul Alinsky-style community organizing groups directly involved with the U.S. street protests, Klein concluded, "(The firm's) fingerprints on promoting and organizing the march bring further evidence suggesting the anti-Wall Street movement is a well-planned campaign and not the spontaneous uprising its leaders claim."

-- Among other America-hating entities that were ultimately revealed to have had more-than-casual connections to the Occupy movement were remnants of the leftist community organization, ACORN; members of the shady Islamist front, CAIR (Council on American-Islamic Relations); the American Nazi Party; and a whole slew of radical reprobates who proudly identify themselves as communists. Not surprising to see Nazis and Islamists involved since much open anti-Semitism was apparent and captured often on camera. Said Glenn Beck, "The 'Marxist Revolution' is an organized effort that is guiding worldwide Occupy protests."

-- Crackerjack conservative Michelle Malkin, my fellow Colorado resident and a diminutive dynamo, who nevertheless takes no quarter from much bigger physical and psychological bullies on the Left, exposed a rent-a-mob scheme among the feckless Fleabaggers. One of the prime examples she cited was a "rented" Hispanic protester during the Occupy D.C. gathering, marching behind a Caucasian individual. Asked why he was there, the Hispanic holding an English protest sign could not articulate what the sign stated. Yet, the radical "ventriloquists" acting as puppeteers stood at the ready to offer their sloganeering-in-unison as to why America is so bad. When Obama won again on Nov. 6, 2012, one of the first things that crossed my mind was the wonderment of how many similar ignoramuses cast their vote for him.

While Obama indeed is the problem, the *real* problem lies in all these cretins who allowed him to be elected twice within a four-year span.

-- An editorial in the *Washington Examiner* correctly surmised, after examining the facts, that the occupiers did not represent Americans or their beliefs. Rather, the editorial, buttressed by the investigative work of one of the paper's reporters, stated that a survey by Richard Stengel's *Time* magazine was intentionally misleading in order to stack facts in the protesters' favor, thus generating misguided sympathy for them. That some of the aforementioned politicians from the so-called mainstream of the Left embraced these scumbags tells me that they themselves are true radicals and no different than the pathetic protesters.

-- You know how lefties always are intoning that it is "for the children"? Well, they are shameless in parading youths in front of the camera for partisan or other philosophical gain. Such was the case with the Fleabaggers, whose pungent "scent" seemed to draw characters of even more dubious distinction than themselves. One Flea Party participant, in Seattle, also the site of another Occupy May Day protest in 2013, was accused of exposing himself to children on several occasions leading up to the Occupy clambake and was arrested for indecent exposure. At one OWS event, radical children's literature was being freely distributed. Moreover, in a really scary scenario, radical Fleabaggers flashed signs advocating beheadings of "white kids," the "hanging" of capitalists to make people "fall in line" and the murder of parents. All this prompted me to ask: "Hey, parents, do you know where your children are right now?"

-- Amid all this weirdness, anti-Americanism and pure sicko conduct, a *New York Post* reporter uncovered a "former hotel chef using only the finest ingredients ... churning out the meals for more than 1,000 protesters every day." I would term a lot of those meals as unjust desserts.

Many of the Occupy protesters have been the Useful Idiots as identified almost a century ago by Vladimir Lenin, or they may have been misled, but idealistic, young people from well-to-do families who find this as their way to rebel. Yet, there are, and have been, those of the same sort whose mission it is to tear down the time-honored traditions of America by revising history to suit their own evil needs. You may or may not have heard of them: Howard Zinn, Noam Chomsky, W.E.B. Du Bois, Oliver Stone, Ed Schultz, Bill Ayers and others. They populate, and predominate in, not only academia, but all the major media outlets, Hollywood and government entities at every level, right up to the most-recent White House and its dishonest and inept top resident. Other than despising and despoiling America in every possible way, the collective goal of these radicals – whether announced or not – is to change documented annals and, in essence, our entire way of life and how we view it; they need to be debunked, and their thoughts deconstructed – which will be accomplished in the pages that ensue.

I entreat people of true faith to pray, over the next three-plus years, that Supreme Court justices Roberts, Scalia, Thomas, Kennedy and Alito remain in good health because if any of them retires or dies, the last nail in the coffin of constitutionality will be hammered into perpetuity by Barack Hussein Obama.

HATING AMERICA

1
HOWARD ZINN AND THE ARAWAKS

In his showcase book, *A People's History of the United States*, first published in 1980 and updated as recently as 2003, Howard Zinn begins with a fixation on raping, enslaving and subjugation of the Arawak tribe in the Bahamas by Christopher Columbus and European explorers in general. Then he systematically transports us through his own unique, and twisted, rendition of American history, right up to the 2000 election and the sea-change from Bill Clinton to George W. Bush.

The U.S. World War II bombardier, who fought Axis encroachment while in uniform, had in all the years since, until his death at age 88 in January 2010, become perhaps the leading radical left-wing voice for changing "history" to suit his own philosophical needs. What is worse than the decided left tilt Zinn took years ago, is that his book has been used in American classrooms as if it were Gospel truth. The book, and similar ones, are far from totally truthful, and are merely the opinions of an elitist and outspoken group of America-haters who would deny our nation's legacy and transform our country into a "utopia" laden with the false promise of a warped, Marxist/Leninist concept called social justice. Although Zinn has since passed on, left in his wake are Barack Obama and other radicals who are intent on wrecking, or despoiling, America.

Zinn unfairly compares the "remarkable . . . hospitality" of the Arawaks, who populated the first islands on which Columbus landed in 1492, with the supposed inhospitability of the Renaissance-Era Europeans. Western Civilization, as a rule, he contends, exhibited a lack of hospitability because it was dominated by papist religionists, monarchial governments and "the frenzy for money." In Zinn's mind, it was cut and dried – no ifs, ands or buts.

However, despite Zinn's obvious distaste, it is an inherent inclination – competition, winners/losers – when humans are pitted *naturally* against each other. That is what has happened as modern civilization and Western movement have evolved: The strong survived, even among so-called native peoples, as more-war-like tribes repeatedly attacked and conquered the more-peaceful ones.

Zinn selectively chooses from Columbus's log to attack the great explorer on point after point – mainly that his discovery of America was merely "lucky," and that he happened upon another land when his intent was to sail to Asia.

Many civilizations, such as those in which most native tribes lived, were inferior by nature because they were communal, counter to man's intuitive desire toward and yearning for private property. Moreover, all of the forward-thinking ideas, later inventions and medical breakthroughs that made life easier for everyone – and helped prolong overall life-expectancy – were generally the result of such factors as competition and markets. This is opposed to the *real* subjugation associated with communal societies: Statism, central planning and social justice (the last merely a euphemism for communist propaganda and indoctrination).

Coupled with all of the socialistic philosophy and applications is overtly centralized education, the result of which has evolved into today's atmosphere where radical thought has run rampant. Of course, Zinn, whose *People's History* frequently shows up – by plan, not accident -- as a "supplemental" textbook in *faux*-history and geography classes such as those of Jay Bennish in Aurora, Colo., is the most characteristic author/example of this phenomenon. His so-called "history" is hundreds of pages that dismantle centuries of genuine, well-documented and sourced history. (There will be a more detailed discussion of radical thinking's negative effect on American education in a later chapter, including more on Jay Bennish and antidotes for parents to combat the onslaught.)

Despite the idealistic and idyllic descriptions of the Arawaks and other communal societies, they were hardly as moral as Zinn portrays them – at least as compared to long-held standards of most God-fearing people. To illustrate his distorted idea of "virtue," Zinn quotes Bartolome de las Casas, a young priest who followed Columbus on seagoing expeditions and later transcribed the Admiral of the Seas' journal in the multi-volume *History of the Indies*. Extolling the fact that the Indians had no religion of which to speak, Zinn includes the following revelatory entry by de las Casas:

> "Marriage laws are non-existent: men and women alike choose their mates and leave them as they please, without offense, jealousy or anger. They multiply in great abundance; pregnant women work to the last minute and give birth almost painlessly; up the next day, they bathe in the river and are as clean and healthy as before giving birth. If they tire of their men, they give themselves abortions with herbs that force stillbirths, covering their shameful parts with leaves or cotton cloths; although on the whole, Indian men and women look upon total nakedness with as much casualness as we look upon a man's head or at his hands."

Amazing. Such a virtuous society admired by Zinn and other fans of atheism, agnosticism and free, unbridled sex. I mean, no marriage laws; no individual parental responsibility; pregnant women working until delivery; abortion-on-demand; and wholesale nudity. Except for the desire for hard work, all of it sounds much like today's permissive and "tolerant" society, which has coincidentally embraced leftist thought processes despite absence of facts other than certain selective reasoning.

Furthermore, in Zinn's book, one would almost expect pornographic illustrations to enhance de las Casas's above descriptions, so as to keep a consistent tone, even for school children, since virtually anything goes when virulent radicals are running the show.

What Zinn does quite often is take anecdotal examples of brutality, slavery and submission by the Europeans over the natives and embellish them well beyond a reasonable point. Even Zinn, in his zeal to revise history, concedes that Columbus's ultimate biographer, the late Harvard historian Samuel Eliot Morison, mentioned these instances. However, the *People's History* author contends that Morison glossed over them to instead emphasize the great explorer's good qualities – which certainly was appropriate on Morison's part.

Zinn equates omission of "facts" to outright lies, yet rather hypocritically admits there is no "intentional deception" on someone like Morison's part. If that is the case, then why basically call Morison a liar? Moreover, Zinn asserts that any so-called de-emphasis of "genocide" can serve "to justify what was done," merely by association.

At virtually every turn throughout American history, Zinn is not only willing – but prefers – to take the side of his self-selected "victims": The Arawaks; slaves; displaced Cherokees; the New York Irish during the Civil War; deserting soldiers in the Mexican War; women workers in non-union mills; the Cubans in the Spanish-American War; socialists in World War I; pacifists in

World War II; and Latin-America *peons* in the post-war "American Empire." It was as if any of these groups NEVER had a voice in genuine historical accounts – which is a folly of fantasy to anyone who has honestly, and unemotionally, assessed U.S. history and its broad-based list of contributors to our melting pot.

Zinn condemns any brutality, alleged or otherwise, by English settlers in early New England as rooted in "civilizations based on private property," his idea no doubt being that, the presence of private landholders inherently, and automatically, foments violence or the darker side of humanity. This is preposterous. Using today's norms as an example, it can be forcefully argued that communities where private property rights are *least* practiced otherwise promote the more-frequent onset of brutality and violence.

Zinn attempts to argue moral equivalence (a favorite ploy of radicals, incidentally) of Josef Stalin's mass murder of Soviet peasants for declared "human progress" with Winston Churchill explaining the bombings of Hamburg and Dresden, and Harry Truman doing likewise regarding Hiroshima. In reality, the Stalinist purges were purely anti-humanity and perpetrated on an innocent, unsuspecting populace in a tightly controlled society; the bombings of Germany and Japan by the Allies were wartime responses to a bellicose "Axis of Evil" and resulted, contrarily, in preventing further unnecessary deaths in an Axis-generated, multi-front war. These Allied actions were typical of those practiced in wars by America and similar, truly free-minded nations.

28

Class warfare, too, is a paramount theme throughout Zinn's writings, not just *A People's History*. Of course, on one side are the "Haves," or "government," or "the rich." Standing steadfastly opposed as "victims" are "the people," a broad-brush definition for *anybody* except, basically, private property owners. If one were to apply the terms used in Ayn Rand's definitive 1957 novel, *Atlas Shrugged*, Zinn's perpetrators, in my mind, would be the producers, while his victims would be the looters. In short, Marxist/Leninist Zinn was a proponent in anti-Randian form of someone who wanted to "take from those according to their ability, and give (read: redistribute) to those according to their need." So, you see, the correlation between the basic types is that trying to change history, in its own way, is a form of redistribution – only what is being *redistributed* are "new truths" by skewing or distorting proven historical facts.

Rather than accept the possibility that native peoples were not the reputed environmentalists for which they are credited, but perhaps instead overgrazed themselves into oblivion over a period of time, Zinn puts them continually on a pedestal by default. In today's climate of rabid environmentalism overcoming all reasonable and proven science with emotional underpinnings, the Left has virtually taken society hostage with its zeal for "change." It could be "protecting" a spotted owl, a snail darter or a brainless tree, but the net effect, of course, is designed to stymie true progress, which carries benefits for all, and transform mankind into a powerless blob controlled by the omnipotent State.

Giving short shrift to a clear historical fact that many slaves were initially captured by fellow blacks in Africa and shipped to the New World, Zinn, as is characteristic with the radical Left, insists that the *real* roots of racism were planted among white American slaveholders. While forcing other human beings into involuntary servitude is indeed heinous and contrary to natural law and individual freedom, there has been a complex set of many other reasons why racism was born.

In yet another preposterous conclusion, Zinn states, as he equivocates about slavery in Africa, "Slavery existed in the African states, and it was sometimes used by Europeans to justify their own slave trade." Citing a book by another apologist, *The African Slave Trade*, by Basil Davidson, he agrees with Davidson that African slaves were more like serfs, who supposedly had some rights. Well, a slave is a slave is a slave – it is all the same. Equivocation in defense of faulty logic is not a virtue.

Admittedly, in the 17th century, in colonies, most notably Virginia and Pennsylvania, indentured servants who were not technically slaves, were not treated well – from the day they boarded crowded, filthy ships to cross the Atlantic. This is indisputable. While Zinn always has blamed "governments" as one of the major bogeymen, laws nevertheless existed to curb excesses against freemen servants; trouble was, they were not always enforced.

Zinn claims roughly one-half of all arrivals in the colonies during the 1600s and well into the 1700s were indentured servants, and some eventually ascended to be landowners, albeit only in the tenant-farmer sense. Because this provided cheap labor for local planters, he attributes it to "clear" evidence of the hardening of class lines. "The distinction between rich and poor became sharper," Zinn asserts.

Could it be, though, that rather than more-defined class lines, there was an increasingly growing and widespread general discontent with the British monarchy, regardless of class status? After all, what resulted by the 1770s was the ultimate watershed of human triumph, the American Revolution. It was an atmosphere not unlike today's, where much of the citizenry feels like indentured servants with a *debt* (double meaning here) to government. (But you say we do not have a monarchy anymore. Then again, do we?) Maybe radicals really meant to say nearly everyone was fed up by then – not just 50 percent of the population.

"The colonies, it seems, were societies of contending classes," Zinn states, "a fact obscured by the emphasis, in traditional histories, on the external struggle against England, the unity of colonies in the Revolution." This emphasis that radicals detest centered on the unity that *naturally* resulted from the creation of a new, free republic, the likes of which has never been replicated, and probably never will be, unfortunately.

The reason traditional histories evolved the way they have was because "we hold these truths to be self-evident," as the Founding documents lucidly declare.

The other issues – to whatever extent they existed – were sidelights to the central struggle against the Crown, and *that* is why original history has been portrayed thusly. Another way to approach it would be that each of the sidelights was thrown into a large cauldron that represented the Revolution, yet none itself was seriously a boiling pot of itself, as Zinn contends.

Zinn believes that the general rebellion would have been decidedly different if Indians, blacks and poor whites had formed a better-organized, combined mini-Revolution of their own, devoid of inclusion of the rest of the population. However, all that falls into the delusional book of "What If?" (which will be covered more thoroughly in a later chapter in this book). It seems in Zinn's conspiratorial mind, the better-off whites who controlled most colonial governments colluded in some manner to prevent such a large, separate insurrection of color and class from occurring. Zinn put it thusly:

> "There still was another control which became handy as the colonies grew, and which had crucial consequences for the continued rule of the elite throughout American history. Along with the very rich and the very poor, there developed a white middle class of small planters, independent farmers, city artisans, who, given small rewards for joining forces with merchants and planters, would be a solid buffer against black slaves, frontier Indians, and very poor whites."

Yet there were concessions to the middle class, he asserts, in order to prolong control over the populace as a whole "without damage to the (ruling class's) own wealth or power, at the expense of slaves, Indians and poor whites," in order to buy loyalty. The device was what he termed the language of liberty and equality as sufficient to unite enough whites. That language twist has turned our current, upside-down society completely on its head, thanks to people like anti-patriotic radical operatives – with political correctness having imposed a suffocating, probably irrevocable, grip on the modern English language.

As he progresses through his perception of America's evolution from an agrarian to industrialized to modern technology-based society, Zinn – wearing thick blinders – presents us with the following faulty conclusions in *A People's History*:

> -- Although abolitionists "did courageous and pioneering work" on trying to eliminate slavery, which Zinn admits, for some strange reason he claims that "blacks had to struggle constantly with the unconscious racism of white abolitionists." This is akin to today's liberals, including the president himself, hollering "racism" anytime someone legitimately dare criticize the administration. I mean, what compels anyone of that ilk to have the gall to imply that *they know* what is inside another person's head or heart? After

all, at their core the average abolitionists were anything but racist. (A separate chapter will cover in-depth the post-Civil War situation of blacks in America and will contrast the thoughtful moderation of Booker T. Washington with the militancy of W.E.B. Du Bois.)

-- Despite ongoing later evidence by reputable, and objective, historians that "robber barons" was an unfair and inaccurate characterization of such late-19th-century industrialists and philanthropists as Andrew Carnegie, Jay Gould, James Mellon and J.P. Morgan, Zinn nonetheless plays the predictable card by blaming them for any inequality or social woes that arose. He is additionally critical of politicians like President Grover Cleveland for encouraging all Americans to become more self-reliant and lean less on government (my, what a horrendous idea).

-- In light of the organized labor-incited Haymarket Square riot in Chicago in 1886, "... the immediate result was a suppression of the radical movement, (but) the long-term effect was to keep alive the class anger of many, to inspire others – especially young people of that generation – to action in revolutionary causes," according to Howard Zinn. These are misstatements of the first order because, while a relatively select few became enmeshed in class consciousness and radical activities, most Americans were not involved in the nascient union push. As I have often conceded – to a point – *some* of the labor unions of the early 20th century were responsible for the advent of the 40-hour week, employee benefits, vacation time and modern child-labor laws. However, many unions otherwise were nothing more than corrupt front groups for American communism. The long-term result of unionism – a somewhat fallacious concept at its core – is that today only about 11 percent of American workers are union members. And most of those belong to public-sector unions wherein the organizations are funded by U.S. taxpayers through involuntary dues that wind up being "laundered" before ultimately landing in the campaign coffers of the Democrat Party. So the myth promulgated by Zinn and others of this supposed revolution of class warfare, coupled with great public zeal for unions, is false.

-- In Zinn's mind, the United States has forever been an expansionist empire, bent on rolling over anything and everything in its path. Lost in this reasoning is the truth and reality of America as a constitutional republic steeped in democratic principles. Regarding the inevitability of Manifest Destiny, radicals of the Zinn variety reject the notion that our nation's growth somehow happened naturally and in a divinely endowed manner. By the early 20th century, as capitalism began to bestow an ever-increasing and justifiable betterment on society, the radicals continued their assault on market forces, opposing "racism, paternalism, and talk of money mingled with talk of destiny and civilization," according to Zinn.

-- A concept called anarcho-syndicalism, as Zinn describes it, took hold first in western Europe. "… The workers would take power, not by seizing the state machinery in an armed rebellion, but by bringing the economic system to a halt in a general strike, then taking it over for the good of all," he states. This "immensely powerful idea," as Zinn terms it, was actually *immensely* bothersome and problematical to average Americans, especially those who never bought into the utopian notion of unions or artificial work stoppages that negatively affected commerce and profits. The ultimate challenge, then, for Zinn and company was to forcefully impose a decidedly socialistic system on the country, defying the God-given thrust of natural law. At about the same time, the Progressive movement was born, eventually, and perhaps unconsciously, lending its name in purloined fashion to present-day liberals and socialists. As I mentioned in the Prologue, however, there is nothing particularly progressive about these types, who more accurately should be called Regressives, in light of their constant thirst for virulent radicalism. Remarkably, Zinn contends that the early Progressives were intent on "fending off socialism" – which I find quite incorrect when the objective record of history is considered in a broader scope.

-- Even though, as we well know, Howard Zinn served honorably in a U.S. uniform during wartime, he nevertheless morphed into one of the nation's primary critics of *any* conflict: Either of the two world wars, Korea, Vietnam, Iraq (and the related War on Terror). Other than writing their own radical volumes on their conceptualization of "history," these often-traitorous and seditious operatives have contributed unnecessarily to much bloodshed among those fighting for freedom by virtue of their heinous activities.

There is one overriding and consistent characteristic that marks the writing of books that radical socialist "historian" Howard Zinn has written over the past four decades or more in bashing America, its military and its foreign policy. With few exceptions, Zinn's default mechanism to cite sources is to use those who are his fellow-travelers – communists or other hard-left ideologues – or organizations that espouse similar, narrow viewpoints. These forces are inherently anti-war and profoundly anti-American; they are classic, and shrill, radicals at heart.

Zinn's work, *Vietnam: The Logic of Withdrawal*, is a case in point. Written first in 1967, when the Vietnam War was beginning to escalate, then re-published in 2002 with updated information – but the same venom and vitriol – the book contains enormous faulty logic and harebrained opinions characteristic of the spiteful, virulent America-hating Left.

Ignoring the fact that the U.S. military, whether on the ground or via air strikes, was routinely hampered and handcuffed by political correctness and poor decision-making by civilians back in Washington, Zinn slams "the most powerful nation in the world." Even though the United States produced "60 percent of the world's wealth, using the most advanced weapons known to military science short of atomic bombs, (it) has been unable to defeat an army of peasants . . ." This is a gross oversimplification. While it is true that, outside of large cities such as Saigon and Hanoi, Vietnam, north and south, was largely an agrarian economy, the war resources of the North Vietnamese Army and Vietcong alike were bolstered by the immense physical firepower and emotional presence of the two communist superpowers of the time, China and the Soviet Union. It was easy for a critic such as Zinn to conclude in 1967, then, that the American bullies were "losing the war."

He contends it was absurd to even think that there were Chinese troops fighting alongside the North Vietnamese and Vietcong, citing that there was no "available evidence" of that. Yet again, please consider that, whether Chinese or Soviet troops were physically present, they certainly were there at least by proxy; I seem to remember having read many reports that each time an American GI died, it was at the hands of AK-47 rifles or other Sino-Soviet weapons. I wonder exactly what "evidence" contrary to that it is which Zinn is talking about.

When he writes that what he calls absurdity is in the mind of the viewer, he is absolutely right, but the absurdity in this case is the constant barrage of leftist drivel that needs to be challenged. Although Zinn's views are grounded in his perception of his own experiences and what he claims is based on data from the public record, I can only faintly concede that he does at least admit some of his conclusions are derived from his own bias – which is considerable. Zinn mentions that he was trained as a historian, but my perception of this man is someone who has been more of a civil-rights activist who turned into an enabler of loudmouth rabble-rousers, not unlike the community-organizer role of Barack Obama. These folks, in essence, are garden-variety America-haters.

If battlegrounds are places of one atrocity after another, which Zinn implies, then all I can say is "war is hell." However, the hell, it seems, always is created in "peacenik" radicals' minds only by America, and *that* should be regarded each time with deep suspicion. In

Zinn's shaky reckoning, there *never* is a valid reason for this country's participation in a war; whomever we are fighting has some moral justification, whereas America lacks any moral justification in every instance and always is guilty of empire-building.

Zinn would rather ignore the mental and physical abuses that have taken place in a less-free society such as China since the Communist Party seized power more than 60 year ago and instead chide the United States. His is a slant that is not uncommon – in U.S. classrooms from kindergarten through the highest university levels. So what we have are not only people with severe left-wing, anti-American viewpoints *allowed* to teach but to monopolize thought in academia.

"American society," he writes, "although it has more freedom of expression than most societies in the world . . . sets limits beyond which respectable people are not supposed to think or speak," using his anti-Vietnam War platform as a launching point for this type of thinking. Except for the truth of the freedom part, all this pretty much is bull because, actually, many limits are imposed by academics, *if* you posit an opposing view.

Interestingly, Zinn developed further perspective to bolster his warped idea of freedom and patriotism by spending some time in Japan in 1966 amid fellow leftists, including trade unionists. Therefore, his vision is shaded by that of Japanese radicals. He quotes one of them, novelist Ken Kaiko, as follows:

"Japanese learned a bitter lesson from fifteen years of fighting on the Chinese mainland: weapons alone are of no avail, in winning the minds and allegiance of any people. … America's conduct of the war in Vietnam is alienating the sympathy of the Japanese."

As the Second Amendment to the U.S. Constitution clearly emphasizes, weapons are indeed of avail to defend one's self. My old boss Ronald Reagan demonstrated how peace through strength can lead to an "Evil Empire's" downfall. By contrast, Zinn and his cohorts regard communism as one of the primary ways "in which underdeveloped countries become organized." I guess by "organized," it means the way unions, communes or other such group-think aggregations organize, in contravention of individual liberty in virtually every instance.

One Marxist Japanese professor quoted by Zinn states: "It is the idea that Communism is the root of all trouble in the world which has brought the Vietnam War." Moreover is a comment by another professor, who earned a doctorate from a major American university: "You can't expect anyone here to take a pro-United States position." These comments are directly in line with Zinn's way of thinking and yet further examples of a wrongheadedness that drives today's radicals.

Another experiential anecdote Zinn uses to buttress his vile views is derived from his days as a civil-rights activist in Mississippi during the height of the Vietnam War. Quoting a black field worker for the radical Student

Non-Violent Coordinating Committee, Zinn says the man told him: "You know, I just saw one of those Vietcong guerrillas on TV. He was dark-skinned, ragged, poor, and angry. I swear, he looked just like one of us." The important point to understand is that this man's prism was not at all that of a black man but more so one merely of any run-of-the-mill anti-war activist, regardless of color. You might call it a basic, knee-jerk, anti-military, anti-American viewpoint.

To prove my point, Zinn, on page after page, employs "stretched" and tortured logic to compare prosecution of the Vietnam War with how blacks were treated in this country. He cites a comment by fellow civil-rights activist Bob Moses, who states: "Our criticism of Vietnam policy does not come from what we know of Vietnam, but from what we know of America." Definitely the epitome of anti-patriotic thought.

Zinn writes that Americans do not burn our history books, yet "our memory sometimes fails us." True, but what is much worse is that virulent radicals willingly ignore what is in those books, then set about to re-write facts to suit their own prejudices against the spirit of the Founders.

Somewhat of an adjunct to both *A People's History* and *The Logic of Withdrawal* is *You Can't Be Neutral on a Moving Train*, published in 1997. In it, Zinn pulls out the class-warfare card again – as is his wont in most of his books anyway – and ties in his annoying agonizing over the Vietnam War with his wonderment as to why there have to be very rich and very poor, often separated by nothing more than a single secret or ivied walls.

Pondering reasons America has been involved in various wars, starting especially in the conflict in which he served, World War II, Zinn produces the following reasons, all hinting at some sort of predictable evil, and all disingenuous as a whole:

> -- A political motive "to demonstrate (to Axis powers) our strength.";
>
> -- "The powerful momentum of a military machine which has been built up and is bursting with energy";
>
> -- "The disinclination to 'waste' a project into which huge amounts of time and money and talent have been expended";
>
> -- "The desire to demonstrate a new weapon";
>
> -- "The cold disregard for human life which develops in the course of a war";
>
> -- "The acceptance of any means, however horrible, once you have entered a war with a belief in the total nobility of your cause."

What is shaky about this multi-point summation, I must remind those who espouse such wrongheaded illogic, is that every major war in which America has been involved in modern times entailed a more-sensible rationale. Either we became enmeshed in hostilities because we were attacked (Pearl Harbor and 9-11), or for humane reasons (to stem the real threat of communist encroachment and prevent the next "domino" from toppling in Korea and Vietnam), or to defend a weaker set of allies (Desert Storm) from neighboring, tyrannical bullies, while ensuring that key world oil supplies are not choked off. It simply is not in Americans' DNA to start wars and to wage them without valid purposes, namely humanitarian or the overall national security and that of the free world as a whole.

In the final section of *You Can't be Neutral*, Zinn laments all the poor souls imprisoned in our country, never admitting that most belong there, whether for more-heinous crimes-against-persons or for quasi-treasonous acts of war protest, as has been the case with his many comrades.

Over the years, Howard Zinn has written numerous other books, all with his special brand of vitriol reserved for the United States, but heaping generous praise on left-wing dictatorships where people have no real rights. Among Zinn's works are *Postwar America: 1945-1971*; *The Politics of History, Terrorism and War*; *The Zinn Reader: Writings on Disobedience and Democracy*; *Howard Zinn on History*; *Howard Zinn on War*; *Three Strikes: Miners, Musicians and Salesgirls*; and *The Unraveling Bush Presidency*. In some cases, as mentioned earlier in this chapter regarding *A People's History*, books by the likes of Zinn and Noam Chomsky (whose anti-Americanism and radicalism I will discuss in the next chapter) are forced upon unsuspecting fertile minds as "supplemental texts" in our schools. If ever you wonder about like-minded thinking and collusive idea-making, stop wondering and consider this: A 2003 biography of Zinn, *Howard Zinn: A Radical American Vision*, was written by his good friend and philosophical soulmate, longtime radical Oklahoma-based professor Davis D. Joyce, with the foreword by Chomsky. Throughout his career of working toward a "vision of a better, more inclusive, and egalitarian, American future," Joyce has practiced a Sooner State-style of historical revisionism, for instance having edited *"An Oklahoma I Had Never Seen Before: Alternative Views of Oklahoma History."*

HATING AMERICA

2

NOAM CHOMSKY AND
ANTI-AMERICANISM
SQUARED

The Massachusetts Institute of Technology, or MIT, as it is more familiarly known, has long cast an aura in my mind of being a learned research setting in Cambridge where the world's brightest minds go to sharpen their intellect, not surprisingly just two miles down Massachusetts Avenue from like-minded, notorious leftist haven Harvard University.

The study of linguistics, to me, always has been a branch of learning wherein these same brilliant students delve into the study of human language, in form, meaning and context, to hone their knowledge further.

Being an American, it has seemed forever, entails proudly possessing a large dose of genuine patriotism and citizenship, enhanced by allegiance "to the flag of the

United States of America and to the republic for which it stands," coupled with a sincere appreciation of our cherished Constitution.

In all these areas, Noam Chomsky has fallen miserably short. Chomsky was a long-term tenured faculty member at MIT, where he technically was supposed to be a linguist before being awarded emeritus status. This has been quite a bit of a charade for some time, however. In reality, Chomsky is a full-blown, professional anti-American, who is not unlike so many other virulent radicals who populate campuses all over the globe. In book after maddening book (he has authored several dozen), Chomsky has given new meaning to the spewing of Marxist venom. But worse yet, he accomplishes this from the font of academia, poisoning fertile young minds as he goes. Such a treasonous creature, though, cannot be blamed singularly for the constant brainwashing of his army of acolytes; no, this process of mind-control begins as early as preschool for most American children. (In a later chapter, I will discuss at length how injection of radical indoctrination is affecting U.S. education, my early background as a teacher offering a springboard for my thoughts.)

Predictably, when the Occupy Wall Street movement began to take shape in the fall of 2011, Chomsky quickly lined up on the protesters' side, calling the protests "an unprecedented opportunity to overcome America's current hopelessness." I agree with him about the hopelessness, but for vastly different reasons. Whatever hope is lacking has been created by the

Fleabaggers' fellow anti-patriots, all the way to the top in the Obama White House; the best single way to revive real hope is at the ballot box in 2014, similar to the populist wave of Tea Party sentiment that swept liberals from Congress in 2010.

On Oct. 22, 2011, Chomsky gave a pep talk to Occupy Boston Flea Party types at their Dewey Square encampment. He freely acknowledged the communal goal of the protests, proclaiming that they "are trying to create cooperative communities that just might be the basis for the kinds of lasting organizations necessary to overcome the barriers ahead and the backlash that's already coming." As he further articulated his reading of the situation at the time, he said "there two real threats to the survival of the human species" – nuclear weapons and environmental catastrophe. Rather than admit that man-made climate change/global warming was essentially a giant hoax perpetrated on the public by "green" whackos like himself, Chomsky attributed "steps backward" by the United States with "openly acknowledged" propaganda by the business community to deny the alleged threat. "The task is not just to understand the world but to change it," he said in directly quoting the co-author of *The Communist Manifesto*, Karl Marx himself. As for the nuclear bogeyman, it is basically a straw figure since in order to revise our past and future, Marxists, of course, fervently believe in *total* disarmament of the populace, save the fascistic rulers who take over after confiscating weapons of all sizes, not just nukes. Chomsky's distaste for the acceptable norms truly is anti-Americanism squared.

The books Noam Chomsky has authored over the years cover a broad gamut of topics, yet ones that no doubt fill the personal libraries of any America-hating, freedom-loathing radical. The subject matter includes nuclear disarmament, gun control, global warming, Palestinian statehood, income redistribution, financial bailouts, U.S. "imperialism" and various crackpot theories as to why the Bush administration conspired to stage the 9-11 attacks to enable a war.

Among Chomsky titles are the following:

> -- *Deterring Democracy* (1991, 1992): The "ruthless" United States, according to the author, creates an international imbalance "to enforce its national interests ... (and) in the process destroys weaker nations."

To refute this thesis, one must first remind Chomsky and his ilk that our country is not a democracy but a constitutional republic grounded in democratic principles. And rather than America being the war-mongering bully roaming the world block, we adhere – in our best fashion – to the idea that, as Theodore Roosevelt famously said, we "speak softly and carry a big stick." There are few, if any, instances in two centuries-plus of existence in which we have unilaterally started a war. Chomsky also carries his anti-war screed a step too far, decrying the War on Drugs as a contrivance to embolden the powers-that-be to "forward the benefits" to other wars.

I would bet that there must be some underlying instruction somewhere in radical leftist teachings that encourages large doses of delusional theorizing.

-- *Chomsky on MisEducation* (2000): Noam Chomsky insists that we must have education reform. I could not agree more. Trouble is, our conceptualizations of what entails reform are at diametrically opposite ends of the spectrum. Like his fellow-travelers who have monopolized the "teaching" process, he believes the problem is far too much input in textbooks from less-than-liberal sources. The reality, as those of us in other camp well know, is the lack of parental choice; the indoctrination of forcing homosexuality, abortion and other aberrant behavior on students; the growing grip that teachers' unions have on education; and far too much political correctness in schoolbooks. A new term to use as code for willy nilly changes in historical content trotted out by the aging radical is "historical engineering," or applying the bias of self-described progressives to traditional education for the purpose of advancing their slant on history. Do not forget that "social justice" always will be an outcome goal for liberals, and Chomsky repeatedly calls for justice in education in *MisEducation*.

-- *Hegemony or Survival: America's Quest for Global Dominance* (2003): Carrying his leftist illogic to the point that he contends the United States is militarizing outer space, Chomsky further accuses our leaders, for the half-century that the Cold War raged, of actively seeking global supremacy. This is in line with the faulty conclusions that America – and *only* America – initiates wars. Every other country (or non-aligned terrorist group, for that matter) naturally is exempt. Remember that murderous, suicidal Islamofascists long ago dubbed us "The Great Satan." In several of his books, including this one, the extremist author/philosopher carries over the message of American "imperial ambitions." It would be easy to presume that left-wing radicals worldwide read Chomsky's ramblings since a constant drumbeat is to always blame the evil Yankee imperialists, even when terrorist attacks are launched with no apparent provocation except animosity *we* purportedly have caused.

-- *Imperial Ambitions: Conversations on the Post-9/11 World* (2005): This volume is a compilation of Colorado-based radical broadcaster/author David Barsamian's interviews with Noam Chomsky in the wake of the worst single man-made tragedy in our nation's history and the resultant, and necessarily responsive, War on Terror. However, rather than express any genuine grief for the thousands of innocent victims of

9-11, Chomsky punches away with his philosophical onslaught aimed at the true forces of good. Ultimately, he actually believes "that a coalition of peace-loving states led by China will coalesce to counter U.S. militarism and aggressiveness." Saying China is peace-loving is like calling Adolf Hitler a kind little man with a funny mustache who loved (non-Jewish) children and dogs.

-- *9-11* (2001, 2002): The Marxist professor emeritus from MIT wrote two editions taking the Bush administration to task on the 9-11 attacks, the first published in 2001, with the update released the following year. In a collection of interviews with him, Chomsky opines that George W. Bush committed criminal acts – not only with such actions as the overall War on Terror and USA PATRIOT Act but conspired with fellow "Neocons" to stage the attacks from within. "The United States continues international terrorism," he states, implying that *we* are the perpetrators, yet ignoring the truth of Islamofascists around the world being the primary launching agents of one deathly terrorist attack after another. In conjunction with the anti-war Ultra-Left's insistence of 9-11 as an inside job, Chomsky offers, "… The World Trade Center attack was a particularly horrifying crime," then adds, "Terrorism, according to the official definition, is simply part of state action, official doctrine," even though with this particular comment he says the United States does not stand alone. To counter this brand of madness, I stood with the ENTIRE U.S. House of Representatives – save misled radical Rep. Barbara Lee, D-Calif. – to vote to approve the Iraq War resolution after 9-11. (Lee will be explored more thoroughly in a later chapter.)

-- *9-11: Was There an Alternative?* (2001, 2002): If he did not drive home his point in the first edition, Chomsky's implication is clear, and inherent in the title, in the follow-up. Alternative, on whose part, I ask. As if our country was in a position to decide regarding an obvious unmitigated surprise attack of gargantuan proportions promulgated by murderous henchmen in the name of a religion with questionable tenets.

-- *Failed States: The Abuse of Power and the Assault on Democracy* (2006): Following up on his 2003 *Hegemony and Survival*, Chomsky further exposes his paranoia about the U.S. interest in "militarizing the whole planet" via military means. No doubt he was not talking about the Obama administration, which announced, the day after the 2012 State of the Union address, the intention for deep, and dangerous, cuts in the military budget. All this while our enemies were laughing behind our backs in anticipation of the decreases and the president's previous

proclamations of specific troop-withdrawal
dates from selected critical theaters of
operation. The *contra* to alleged militarization
and empire-building, Chomsky reasons with
characteristic illogic and jingoism, is
democracy "at home and abroad." Yet, by
democracy, he means, more accurately, the
radical version, or that with a strong dose of
"social justice." This prescription includes
relying on world courts, not the U.S.
Constitution; letting the United Nations "lead
in international crises"; using diplomatic,
rather than military, resolution of threats; and
signing and carrying forward the faulty,
costly Kyoto protocols.

-- *Gaza in Crisis* (2010): Written with fellow
radical academic Ilan Pappé, the book,
subtitled *Reflections on Israel's War Against
the Palestinians*, is another disingenuous
attempt by our homegrown, internal enemies
to portray Israel as the bully who initiates
unprovoked hostilities. As Ronald Reagan
reminded presidential debate opponents who
played fast and loose with facts, "There you
go again." How delusional can one be in light
of Palestinian miscreants lobbing rockets
across at Israelis on an almost-daily basis, and
Israel only responding to such cross-border
misbehavior? Chomsky and his co-author
fervently believe that only a "two-state
solution" is workable, and the former is
pessimistic that Middle East peace is feasible.

Tell that to the Palestinians who insist on war-mongering in conjunction with the Muslim concepts of *jihad* and the wholesale destruction of the State of Israel.

-- *Hopes and Prospects* (2010): Carrying his ultra-leftist philosophical bent beyond Palestine, Israel and Mediterranean shores, Noam Chomsky challenges American Exceptionalism, the War on Terror and its multiple fronts, along with financial bailouts, and cheerleads for a perceived democratic" wave in Latin America. However, his idea of democracy in our hemisphere is more along the lines of Castro's Cuba or the late Hugo Chavez's Venezuela – such fertile fonts of freedom. Not.

-- *Making the Future: The Unipolar Imperial (2011):* In his latest assault on our sensitivities, Chomsky relentlessly continues his message that the United States is the world's bad boy, interested only in imperialistic expansion. If he is hard on his fellow Marxists in the White House, it is only because he incredibly believes Barack Obama and his inner circle are not far enough to the left. That trite term, "social justice," has basically been supplanted by a new twist, "social welfare." Chomsky also reiterates his slant or introduces fresh radical fodder on such other topics as the ongoing financial crisis, the limits of the two-party system,

> nuclear Iran, Afghanistan, Israel-Palestine,
> corporate power and the general future of
> American politics. As disconcerting as it was
> to read his past ravings, this latest monstrosity
> is perhaps the most-difficult to swallow.

Alan Dershowitz, a noted left-wing lawyer and academic, is someone with whom I never agree, except on the issue of Israel's right to exist and the Jewish state's critical and strategic location. In May 2011, Dershowitz wrote an op-ed column at *Newsmax.com* criticizing Chomsky's defense of Osama bin Laden after brave U.S. Navy SEALS killed the terrorist mastermind in Pakistan.

Harvard's Dershowitz quickly responded to Chomsky's description of bin Laden as an innocent victim of "cold-blooded murder," terming the fellow Cambridge-based radical's comments as "shameful." Chomsky had made his ill-advised remarks despite bin Laden's "own admission of complicity in the murder of 3,000 people. ....," Dershowitz wrote. "... Nor does he believe the evidence gathered by the 9/11 Commission, the grand jury that indicted bin Laden, the numerous confessions and claims of responsibility by al-Qaida Operatives, and the video showing those who flew the planes in the presence of Osama bin Laden and Ayman al-Zawahiri."

Chomsky, a Jew by birth, also is excoriated in the same column by Dershowitz, also Jewish, for "writing in defense of Holocaust denier Robert Faurisson's claim that the so-called Holocaust was a fraud perpetrated by the

Jewish people." In the MIT academic's bizarre reasoning, Chomsky said that "nobody believes (there is) an anti-Semitic connotation to the Holocaust ... whether one believes it took place or not."

Wrote Dershowitz, hardly a conservative himself, "I have debated Chomsky on several occasions and have found that he simply makes up facts and then characterizes them as 'uncontroversial.' This tactic works with sycophantic college audiences on the hard left, but ... anyone who bothers to check 'Chomsky facts,' as his critics aptly dub them, will find that the source is often conspiratorial websites and hate propaganda."

Just remarkable, a committed liberal of one stripe going after one of another ilk altogether. However, it is precisely the kind of thinking that ranks Noam Chomsky right at the top of the list of virulent, freedom-hating, America-despising radicals, right next to his late, close friend, Howard Zinn.

3

W.E.B. DU BOIS
AND THE RACE HUSTLERS

While Howard Zinn can be regarded as the genuine "godfather" of the historical revisionists, then similar status for what I term the Black Grievance Movement must be bestowed upon neither Jesse Jackson nor Al Sharpton nor even the late Malcolm X. No, that "honor" was earned long ago by William Edward Burghardt Du Bois, who was born just after the Civil War and died at age 95, ironically just a day before Martin Luther King Jr.'s 1963 "I Have a Dream" speech. W.E.B. Du Bois was the original Pan-Africanist and racial separatist in the early 1900s.

If Dr. King were still alive and observing today's political theater, he would be writing a speech entitled, "I have a nightmare." The American left, fueled by latter-day reverse racists who are the heirs to Du Bois's dubious legacy, has transformed King's struggle for equal rights into a race to the bottom in political ethics. The 2012 election season demonstrated that the shameless abuse of the allegation of "racist" against opponents of the leftist agenda knows no bounds.

A recent high-profile victim was the new Republican U.S. senator from South Carolina, Tim Scott. Scott is a former U.S. representative appointed to the post by South Carolina Gov. Nikki Haley and is the first black U.S. senator from the South since Reconstruction. But he is "not black enough" for professors at Harvard and the guardians of civil-rights orthodoxy in the news media.

Welcome to the Orwellian world of American politics. In our new politically correct universe, a public official will be labeled racist if he opposes racial quotas, and he will be called "anti-civil rights" if he wants only warm-body citizens to vote, not cemetery residents. And, he will be smeared as "anti-immigrant" if he does not think illegal aliens should be voting in local school board elections. Shades of Du Bois, indeed.

Du Bois's original thoughts are contained in a book, which he chronicled first in 1903, then which was re-published in 1976, 13 years after his death in Ghana, where he moved and became a citizen while never renouncing his U.S. citizenship. *The Souls of Black Folk* contains 16 essays and sketches by Du Bois; it was largely meant to be a challenge to black self-help pioneer and philosophical arch-rival Booker T. Washington, and sums up Du Bois's beliefs just after the turn of the 19th into the 20th century.

He admits evolving into a belated admirer of Karl Marx and reflects on how Communism's founder put his thoughts into action by co-authoring *The Communist*

Manifesto with Friedrich Engels. Moreover, by the mid-1900s, Du Bois shares his fondness and admiration for Soviet tyrant Josef Stalin, whose bloodlust resulted in more deaths of his countrymen than anyone in history, including such prolific megalomaniacs as Adolf Hitler, Mao Zedong and Pol Pot.

Conceding that "to me the color line is a great problem of this century," Du Bois proclaims "a greater problem" is that "so many civilized persons (read: white racists, or mainly *all* whites) are willing to live in comfort even if the price of this is poverty, ignorance and disease of the majority of their fellowmen" (a hard-rock socialistic viewpoint for sure). Then he proceeds with predictable anti-war invective, contending that "the excuse for this war continues largely to be color and race." These general pronouncements, remarkably made when we were *not* involved in any war – in the period between the Spanish-American War and World War I -- provide a wide window into the "soul" of Du Bois, who likely would be comfortable among Jackson, Sharpton and today's other virulent race hustlers and shakedown artists. These views also validate Du Bois' status as one of the original 20th-century Marxists, the racial aspect notwithstanding.

More astounding to me, before considering any elaboration of his philosophies, is that W.E.B. Du Bois was neither a product of an urban ghetto nor a rural cotton field; he was born and reared in a bucolic village in southwestern Massachusetts's Berkshire Hills, hard by the

New York border. The ugly specter of racial prejudice certainly always has existed in various, and sometimes unlikely, quarters. However, I find it incredible that seeds for his ultimate leftism were sowed in the quietude of the rolling New England hills, unless he had too much time on his hands as a child so as to let his imagination run as wild as the animal population in those nearby little mountains.

Du Bois's initial realization that he was somehow different was apparent early in his grammar-school years through what he terms "double-consciousness," or living in one (white) world but being considered as part of another (black). "One ever feels his two-ness, -- an American, a Negro; two souls, two thoughts, two unreconciled strivings, two warring ideals in one dark body, whose dogged strength alone keeps it from being torn asunder," he writes. In my mind, this philosophy in many ways is what is wrong with contemporary America – a morally rudderless ship far out at sea tossed about by giant waves of discontent, punctuated by vile pronouncements of hyphenated-this and separatist-that.

"The history of the American Negro is the history of this strife. ...," Du Bois states, then goes on to lament, via a laundry list, the woes of why one's merely being "a Negro" automatically closes "the doors of opportunity" and therefore justifies an antidote of rampant socialism and attendant redistribution.

It is indeed tough in America to overcome racism and other man-made obstacles, but because, contrarily, it is America, the doors of opportunity, although sometimes closed, are not locked, provided an individual possesses the inner-zeal to try and open them. In Du Bois's mindset, however, only the "good hand of government" is a requisite for opening any of these doors. The door analogy is apt because liberals/socialists rarely bust down portals (unless they physically riot); instead they enter toe-by-toe until their feet, and ultimately their entire bodies, are completely in the room they wish to rearrange.

In the half-century that passed since the end of American slavery and until the time Du Bois began more openly presenting his view more publicly, great strides were made by blacks as a free people. Nevertheless he declares in *Souls* that "the freedman has not yet found freedom in his promised land. Whatever of good may have come in these years of change, the shadow of a deep disappointment rests upon the Negro people. ..." Blaming war, the Ku Klux Klan, "the lies of carpetbaggers" and "the disorganization of industry" as hurdles, Du Bois nonetheless concedes that the 15th Amendment at least provided basic voting rights.

Responsible for a larger-than-normal rate among blacks over two centuries of children born out of wedlock, according to Du Bois, were "white adulterers, threatening almost this obliteration of the Negro home." In other words, even though we know, as the old saying goes, "it takes two to tango," he sees no need for any sharing of this responsibility; blacks, in his mind, will always be victims but never abettors or perpetrators.

As a solution to all these problems, Du Bois advances the idea of racial separatism – hinting that only blacks can truly solve "Negro" problems, unless, of course, there is a benevolent, omnipotent government to serve as an in-lieu "nanny," regardless of race.

Du Bois is so cynical about race issues that, like voting rights finally granted to blacks, he claims the Emancipation Proclamation "seemed but to broaden and intensify the difficulties." This man never was satisfied with even the most-minute post-slavery progress, being so hell-bent on advancing a them-vs.-us posture, as evidenced by his lifelong, separatist and Pan-African zeal.

Du Bois demonstrates a curious stance about educating the freed blacks: "The opposition to Negro education in the South was at first bitter, and showed itself in ashes, insult, and blood; for the South believed an educated Negro to be a dangerous Negro. And the South was not wholly wrong; for education among all kinds of men always has had, and always will have, an element of danger and revolution, of dissatisfaction and discontent." Then he hits on a key point by adding, "Nevertheless, men strive to know." What is critical about this paradox is that, to this day, in the poorest black enclaves, government has denied parents choice in their children's education – whether vouchers or tuition tax credits to enable them to select a specific school rather than be forced to accept a subpar neighborhood location that masquerades as a learning center. This denial of choice has been central to the overall philosophy of Du Bois and other revisionists.

In what Du Bois characterizes as "unwritten history" – taking yet another stab at revising the books – he chides the government-blessed creation, and eventual failure, of the Freedmen's Bank and related savings banks after the Emancipation Proclamation for throttling any potential financial progress of freed slaves. "Where all the blame should rest is hard to say," he declares. "Whether the (Freedmen's) Bureau and the bank died chiefly by reason of the blows of its selfishness or the dark machinations of its foes, perhaps even time will never reveal." To me, though, the 1860s atmosphere suspiciously resembles more-recent financial failures – fueled by government intervention and central control – such as the Dot.Com Bubble, Fannie Mae, Freddie Mac and the entire mortgage crisis.

En toto, what Du Bois advocated was an actualization of his own pipe-dreams of separate and well-delineated societies, one black, one white. He had no delusion of integration or intermingling, except on selected, rare issues that suited his social-engineering purposes. For instance, his separatist and revisionist policy vision included "a permanent Freedmen's Bureau, with a national system of Negro schools; a carefully supervised employment and labor office; a system of impartial protection before the regular courts; and such institutions for social betterment as savings-banks, land and building associations, and social settlements." Implementation of these facets would have "solved in a way we have not yet solved the most perplexing and persistent of the Negro problems." In other words, this agenda incorporates segregated education, government-generated jobs, liberal judicially active courts, so-called socially responsible investment avenues and communal residences – a blueprint with a decidedly Marxist footprint if ever there was one. Many of the problems we face generally as a society and culture today, though, are an unsavory and unfortunate byproduct of this line of thinking.

After offering early token praise for Booker T. Washington, writer, inventor and founder of Alabama's Tuskegee Institute (which later produced the fabled and highly decorated Airmen squadron in World War II), Du Bois proceeds to heap on criticism of the premier black pacesetter of the 19th century. Whether out of jealousy, or perhaps because conservatives were among the legions who admired Washington over the years, Du Bois employs back-door and backhanded terminology to assess the former's lifelong achievements. When addressing Washington's "misstatements and shortcomings ...as well as his triumphs ...," Du Bois reckons that "it is easier to do ill than well in the world." Hardly a hearty endorsement of the enormous good Washington accomplished, and very much like the attacks on a modern-day conservative like South Carolina senator Scott, who had the audacity to be born black.

"... Among his own people ... Mr. Washington has encountered the strongest and most-lasting opposition," especially with educated blacks, manifested in "a feeling of deep regret, sorrow, apprehension at the wide currency and ascendancy which some of Mr. Washington's theories have gained." Du Bois believed that Washington placed too much emphasis on industrial education, instead encouraging blacks to give up political power, insistence on civil rights and higher education of black youth. Such an agenda is not totally impractical, as we could use *less* insistence on "civil rights" these days, plus some otherwise-good students simply do not see college in their future and would rather work in a high-paying trade of some sort. Yet many high-school counselors are literally forcing some young people into college preparatory courses when they should be steering them more conscientiously into maybe an industrial arts or other direction. I recall No. 1 radio talker Rush Limbaugh, who is a very bright man, often talking about coming from a long line of lawyers but being bored in high school and wanting only to be a radio personality. Then he purposely flunked out of the small state college in his southeastern Missouri hometown, immediately carving out his dream – and the rest is history. Plus, GOP presidential hopeful Rick Santorum in February 2012 echoed Washington's theme when he rightly criticized President Obama for seemingly channeling Du Bois's insistence that it was college education-or-nothing for all, even prospective tradesmen, craftsmen or various artists who have no necessity for traditional college and its attendant, common-place academic brainwashing.

Du Bois goes far to imply that, over the years, Washington's harshest critics have been continually chastised and hushed up, which Du Bois calls "the social student's inspiration and despair. … Mr. Washington represents in Negro thought the old attitude of adjustment and submission. …" According to Washington's most-severe critic, the three "Negro" trends that have occurred are the disenfranchisement of blacks, legal creation of civil inferiority for blacks and a steady withdrawal of aid from institutions for "higher training of the Negro." Considering all of this, it seems like faint praise when Du Bois actually extols any of the positive accomplishments of Booker T. Washington.

Finally, Du Bois says, Washington "is especially to be criticised (sic)" for "his doctrine (tending) to make the whites, North and South, shift the burden of the Negro problem to the Negro's shoulders and stand aside as critical and pessimistic spectators." To which I would retort that the real pessimism lies in the minds of revisionists like Du Bois and his fellow-travelers.

According to Du Bois, European civilization among undeveloped peoples "certainly forms a chapter in human action not pleasant to look back upon. War, murder, slavery, extermination, and debauchery, -- this has again and again been the result of carrying civilization and the blessed gospel to the isles and the heathen without the law." Such an attitude is characteristic of Marxist ideology and its overall contempt of religion and European influence. It also represents a general abrogation of responsibility that monopolizes liberal thought and is therefore a key component of revisionism. Du Bois dismisses advocacy of this type of thinking by referring to European rule as "a triumph of brute force and cunning over weakness and innocence." I will say clearly that *no* society in all of history has an exclusive ownership of either brutal domination or benign innocence, as Du Bois implies.

Du Bois cites the primary reasons for many decades of an inordinately high crime rate in the black community as being the Emancipation Proclamation, followed not long afterward by post-Civil War Reconstruction, reckoning in his own mind that the sudden leap from slaves to freedmen caused a long-term serious problem that in actuality has been fueled by numerous complex issues. "The inevitable result of Emancipation was to increase crime and criminals," he states. "… The appearance of the Negro criminal was a phenomenon to be awaited." Again, my take is, we *all* are responsible for our own actions, regardless of the hand dealt to each of us; from a psychoanalytical standpoint, there can be no boiler-plate excuse whatsoever for aberrant behavior by any group.

One thing becomes quickly and automatically clear about Gerald Horne, who wrote the 2010 biography, *W.E.B. Du Bois*: Horne is of the same ilk as his subject, philosophically and socio-economically. For instance, from the outset, Horne specifically cites two extreme-leftist scholars, Herbert Aptheker and David Levering Lewis, as his exemplars, not only because they also wrote biographies of Du Bois, but due to their shared distaste for almost anything American. In his previous books, Horne, an African-American Studies professor at a historically black university in Texas, has had a penchant, like Barack Obama, for playing the race card to the hilt, whether it applied to politics, economics, war, or virtually any other issue. In short, Gerald Horne is the ideal Du Bois biographer --- like his hero, he perfectly channels the original race-baiter by despising anything truly worthwhile about America.

In Horne's biography, he details the episode wherein Du Bois supposedly is considered for the top post in the Washington, D.C., public schools just after the turn of the 20th century. However, according to Horne, the possibility was jettisoned by Booker T. Washington. "A simmering conflict between these two men was now metastasizing into a boiling and rancorous dispute, the ramifications of which were to shake America for decades to come," Horne writes, laying any any general future woes by blacks directly, and only, at Washington's feet. But when I assess the overall track record of a uniter like Washington compared to a divider like Du Bois, I find this type of piling-on hard to accept on its face.

Racial turmoil in 1906 accelerated Du Bois's further downward spiral deep into collectivist thinking. As Horne puts it, "… He endorsed government ownership of railroads, coal mines, and certain factories. As he saw it then, in the 'socialistic' trend … lies one great hope of the Negro American." It was at the same time that Du Bois began a lifelong membership in the Socialist Party, which to me offers strong testimony as to his virulent anti-American leanings.

Like today's self-described "progressives," Du Bois rationalized that the then-Democratic Party, despite its alliance with such white-purity groups as the Ku Klux

Klan, was better for blacks than the GOP because of the latter party being less hostile to "monopolies and imperialism," as Horne writes. Of course, while the Republican Party always has its warts, it is, at least ideally, a bastion of individual liberty, free markets and protean national defense – something which Du Bois either never understood, or never admitted, in his 90-plus years of life.

Another characteristic W.E.B. Du Bois shared with today's socialists and Marxists was the repeated ability to convene with others of a like mind to "solve" America's problems. Trouble is, they *always* have done this on foreign shores, or even in Canada – perhaps because either, figuratively or literally, they have felt some sort of immunity from prosecution, or at least from immediate and direct criticism from their own countrymen. Over the years, Du Bois's itinerary read like a travelogue of anyplace but the United States: London, Berlin, Paris, Amsterdam, Ghana and just across the Canadian border in Niagara Falls, Ontario. Horne thoroughly discusses the Du Bois foreign forays, with much empathy at every turn.

If ever there was any doubt about Du Bois's sympathies, Horne dispels that notion with the following declaration regarding his biographical subject's activities after World War I and leading into World War II more than two decades later:

"With aching precision, Du Bois took to the pages of the mainstream press to plead on their behalf but at a certain point he had to wonder if justice could actually be found in a nation founded on the principle of enslavement of Africans."

The specific group to which Horne refers comprised black sharecroppers in Arkansas who were either slaughtered or others who were jailed when they protested their plight in the cotton fields.

Of Du Bois's scholarly activity as he approached age 70, Horne surmises, rather solicitously and incorrectly, "Through diligent research and a visceral rejection of the racist stereotypes that too often characterized the writing of U.S. history, Du Bois emblazoned a new trail of scholarship that continues to reverberate and, in some ways, his efforts have revolutionized the historical profession itself." Any revolutionizing that resulted, I think, was due to "historiography," or study of history through ultra-critical means rather than factual face-value, and obviously had a negative effect, as evidenced by all the revisionists over the years who followed Du Bois, whether black, white or from some other ethnic group.

Similar to Booker T. Washington, but in a different vein, quite the antithesis to W.E.B. Du Bois was William Wilberforce, a Member of Parliament in Britain. Wilberforce, who died in1833, long before either Du Bois or Washington was born, is credited by fair-minded people with ending slave trade. However, it is unlikely one will find him in history books because he did it as an evangelical Christian – quite an unfashionable stance, especially to historical revisionists.

TOM TANCREDO

Capturing the essence of Wilberforce, though, have been two biographies, both published in 2007. Although they vary in approach, the two volumes give this great, selfless man – who also happened to be white -- his proper due. One, *William Wilberforce: The Life of a Great Anti-Slave Trade* Campaigner, was written by William Hague, most recently a British MP and Foreign Secretary who previously served as a Shadow Cabinet Member and once was Conservative Party leader. The other, *The Amazing Grace of Freedom: The Inspiring Faith of William Wilberforce, the Slaves' Champion*, was co-authored by three Hollywood conservatives, Ted Baehr, and the husband-wife team of Susan and Ken Wales.

Despite the aforementioned earlier mention of Du Bois's unfair criticism of abolitionists in general, it is quite clear in both biographies that Wilberforce continually used his faith to propel his best efforts to try and effect worldwide abolition of slavery.

Bearing further testimony to many blacks' gratitude, albeit belated, to William Wilberforce was the creation in 1856 of one of the few historically black colleges north of the Mason-Dixon Line, and the nation's first private black college, southwestern Ohio's Wilberforce University. (Ironically, when you consider the philosophical differences between him and the great British abolitionist, Du Bois was a professor at the university for two years in the 1890s.)

HATING AMERICA

The next time you hear any of the liberal revisionists – especially the ones who routinely play the race card, whether it be Jesse Jackson, Al Sharpton, Cornel West, Tavis Smiley, or whomever – keep in my mind that their yelling and screaming has its roots more than a century ago in W.E.B. Du Bois.

4

OLIVER STONE AND THE "HOLLYWOOD CHARACTERS"

Even though they are both 60-something Baby Boomers, there is no more stark contrast in the entertainment community than that of Oliver Stone and David Mamet, two of Hollywood's most creative minds. Stone fought as a U.S. Marine in Vietnam, then took a decidedly left turn in his public views and filmmaking, which definitely reflect large tinges of Marxism and even paranoia. Mamet, conversely, had been what he terms a "brain-dead liberal" throughout most of his 30-year-plus moviemaking and playwriting career – before his conversion not long ago to a champion of traditional values.

In the weird world of Tinseltown, it is an exception if you are not a liberal, especially if you appear on-screen. It also is a badge of honor that you prove to your peers you are capable of challenging and contradicting conventions of culture, most notably if anti-American and anti-conservative criticism accompanies your act. The most-common practitioners, of course, are actors, who study their lines and follow the dictates of directors. They are true "Hollywood characters."

One will find fewer film directors who publicly and directly excoriate this country and its founding principles; rather they accomplish *their* deed by using the actors, the compliant grunts, to convey the message through scripts. An exceptional case among directors is Oliver Stone; in addition to transmitting anti-American vibes via his actors, Stone is quite outspoken in the same vein with his public statements. For years, he has openly embraced such brutal dictators as Fidel Castro and the late Hugo Chavez, yet, to hear Stone tell it, someone like George W. Bush is the epitome of evil. Which is all the more remarkable considering Stone grew up as the only child in a reputedly conservative, two-parent family on the East Coast before his Vietnam stint in the military.

The best way to analyze Stone is to delve deep into the writings of those who have assessed his work or interviewed him extensively, such as professors Don Kunz and Charles L.P. Silet. Kunz edited a 1997 book, *The Films of Oliver Stone*, in which the University of Rhode Island academic compiled a collection of essays about, and interviews with, Stone. Silet, a faculty member at Iowa State University, edited the 2001 *Interviews with Oliver Stone*, in which Silet tied together sit-downs by various interviewers with the controversial filmmaker. When you sift through the entirety of Kunz's compilation, you find a portrait of a complex creator/commentator – the main *caveat* being that it is done through the prism of Stone's fellow lefties. So one finds it difficult to swallow without the proverbial grain of salt.

In his preface, Kunz states that Stone's movies always tend to "focus on an angry male protagonist pursuing a redemptive quest that is at once personal and national, and which display technological flamboyance. This is to say that his body of work has been in the public interest, deeply felt on a personal level, and stylishly innovative." I tend to both agree and disagree, for different reasons. First, I believe most of Stone's films are transferrals of emotion from himself to the characters he has cast – in other words, a lot of autobiographical depictions shrouded in the *dramatis personae* of fictional anti-heroes. Second, my disagreement with Kunz lies in his statement about "public interest." Because it is obvious to me that Stone's efforts are largely counter to the genuine public interest. While the projects entertain – from a typically left-wing perspective and in strictly an amusement sense – they are nonetheless watched, at least the original English-language versions, by an American film-going populace that has been proven, in poll after poll, to have a center-right bent. Therefore, I often have wondered how the average patriotic American *really* feels about Stone's animus toward this country, and whether Joe Moviegoer is willing to accept these films strictly for entertainment and shock value, or to buy into the Stone insistence that the celluloid depictions represent actual history.

Stone's films are, in my view at least, quite often anti-patriotic screeds rife with paranoia, distorted visions of what America really is, and has been, and negativism. *JFK, Platoon* and *Nixon* are instances of delusional conspiracy theories intermingled with vast mental problems of those portrayed. All this, naturally, is technically fiction, yet I firmly believe many of these tales are actually fictionalized *memoirs* in one sense or another, even though the director would want us to believe it is unvarnished history – from his bizarre perspective. Another perplexing aspect of this enigmatic man to me is his pronounced anger toward "Jewish domination" of Hollywood; it is puzzling because Stone, although reared as an Episcopalian who now practices Buddhism, is the son of a Jewish father.

Key characters in Stone creations – *Platoon, Natural Born Killers* and *Born on the Fourth of July* – lend credence to what in my mind is obvious, and which seems reinforced by Kunz as well. In his preface, the Rhode Island professor declares: "Perhaps these three characters are stand-ins for Stone himself, the Vietnam veteran returned from the brink of the grave to write, direct, and produce the postmodern horror film called *revisionist American history*" (my italic emphasis added). There you have it – an evaluator not necessarily hostile to Oliver Stone calling him exactly what the director is.

"The celluloid stories Stone tells are clearly designed to convince Americans of the need for social and political change, to shock them, to rouse them from their lethargy, to terrify them, make them angry, incite them to act. His cinematic techniques serve those ends," Kunz writes. In other words, through his on-screen work,

78

coupled with his overt political alliances, Stone has become a Marxist enabler who stokes the fires of anti-Americanism and severe revisionism. Thus, his final product is undoubtedly a contribution to the confused society his ilk have helped formulate.

Stone does go out of his way to cast America in a negative light. To wit, according to Kunz, "(Stone is) willing to risk new ways of persuading audiences to accept uncomfortable ideas about themselves *and their nation*" (again my italic emphasis added). In advancing all his shadowy portrayals of a darker, less-charitable America, Stone always is willing to push the envelope. For instance, in *JFK,* his movie on the Kennedy assassination in Dallas in 1963, he apparently has convinced sympathetic reviewers that the content was more historical fact than fictionalized concoction distilled from history. According to Kunz in his preface, Robert A. Rosenstone "defends Stone's most controversial film against the widespread charge that it has twisted history." Rosenstone's critique (which is part of the Kunz book) is titled *JFK: Historical Fact/Historical Film,* as if such a conclusion is a settled issue, which, of course, it is not, and likely never will be.

A multi-session, December 1990 interview of Stone by poet/novelist/music producer David Breskin is included in Kunz's book. Breskin plays amateur psychologist, asking the director numerous in-depth questions tracing back to his childhood, his tenuous relationship with his father, his parents' mutual infidelity and their eventual divorce. Stone's answers reveal a complex *persona* interspersed with inbred anger and elaboration on his *raison d'etre*, yet punctuated by a lusty sense of humor. (The dark, wry humorous side emerges at the most-unexpected points of Stone's films, amid all the controversy, violence, sex and paranoid visions of the America – or world – he perceives.)

Quoting Stone, Breskin writes about the former's realization – in *Stone's* head – that he had qualms about the war, and Washington, early on. "... I knew something was off in Vietnam, and I knew that the government was really shi—ing us, but I didn't know exactly how," Stone related. "My rage was such that I knew something was wrong. And I thought, let's do the government, let's take it down. What's the big deal? Let's go to Washington with some rockets and some mortars and f---ing fight. And we can win it. I just didn't like all the talk, all that hippie bullsh---. ..."

In the Breskin interview, Stone refers to a quote by Richard Boyle, the main character in a political movie he wrote and directed, *Salvador*, and admits he agrees with the sentiment expressed: "I believe in America. I believe I stand for something. For a constitution, for human rights, not just a few people, but for everybody on this planet." And that sentiment is precisely the problem with Stone's depiction of "Americanism"; we cannot, and should not, be caretakers for the rest of the world. Moreover, when trouble occurs elsewhere, it is not appropriate for the likes of Stone to blame our country for the world's woes.

Breskin asks Stone if he would "favor continually remythologizing American history because we need a better 'good' to believe in than the one that we have?" To which, the director replies: "Yes. That's a good point. But at the same time, a balance: You show the truth but you try to show a goodness in the truth, too." However, I ask, where is much genuine goodness in Stone's films and where is this supposed balance to which he refers?

David Sanjek, a left-tilting music archivist and film-studies teacher at New York City's Marxist-leaning New School, analyzes Stone in a chapter titled *The Hysterical Imagination: The Horror Films of Oliver Stone*. The title exists because the director's earliest, less-famous films, dating back to the early 1970s, were of the horror genre. Transferral again is important, Sanjek contends, due to the manner in which Stone has leapt emotionally by continuing to utilize forms of horror as vehicles in his later, better-known works. Rather than horror, I would classify the latter more as horrific in the dishonor and disingenuousness they offer.

In contrast to previous pastoral settings, Sanjek writes, in most of Stone's movies, "The city ... is portrayed as alienating and corrupting ... (or) an environment in which men lose their power and their function. These patterns appear later in Stone's work, as one associates the predominantly urban environments of *Wall Street*, *Talk Radio*, the suburban and hospital sequences of *Born on the Fourth of July*, and the governmental and legal locations of *JFK* with the nightmare of incipient fascism of the expression of hegemonic control.

"Any time Stone addresses complex social and political issues, he reduces the material to a war of conflicting moral points of view that obfuscates much of their ideological content." While this is at least partially true, let me reiterate that, when I watch a Stone film, I mostly glean from the viewing a clear and specific viewpoint – that of a filmmaker bent on historical revisionism.

Sanjek emphasizes that Stone "clearly has a selective and overly romantic view of American history." Stone certainly is selective in arbitrarily choosing what *is* and *is not* an accurate rendition of history. This is reinforced in another book, the 1995 *Past Imperfect: History According to the Movies*, with Mark C. Carnes the primary editor; in it is included a conversation between author/history professor Eric Foner and another noted Hollywood director, John Sayles. In analyzing Stone's *JFK*, Sayles captures the totality of Stone by saying, " … One of the things (Stone) did was hit you with so many images so quickly --- some of them familiar, some of them new information – in such a barrage of documentary styles that he was able to pass off stuff that was fairly speculative. …"

In a discussion of Vietnam movies by former war correspondent Frances FitzGerald later in the Carnes-edited book, the journalist also is on target echoing a similar sentiment: "Oliver Stone's *Platoon* begins with an extraordinary, hyper-real evocation of jungle warfare, but then the film descends into facile mythmaking – and at the same time departs from its particular landscape." I find it incredible that even these interviewers who typically share Stone's warped worldview still do not have to reach far to conclude he has little trouble convincing himself of the blurred line between actual history and his fictional conceptualization of it.

Silet's compilation book includes interviews with Stone by a dozen different questioners over the years, many somehow reaching like-minded realizations to the conclusions of others who have spent lengthy sessions with the director. For instance, *Cineaste* editor Gary Crowdus, three of whose sit-downs with Stone are in the Silet volume, explores Stone's political views and his dramatic license in two separate chapters. Yet, while Crowdus exhibits perhaps the most-sympathetic slant toward the controversial director, he still is able to elicit the unsavory consistency of Stone's views – and willingness to bend history for revision's sake. Defining dramatic license, in response to Crowdus's question, Stone states, "… (It is) a restaging of any reported action – reported, *not necessarily factual* (my italics again) – using actors, costumes, make-up, the condensation of events, and the invention of dialog(ue) which occurred behind closed doors, to illustrate your conception of what occurred."

(A maybe not-so-remarkable event occurred in February 2012 – when you consider the perils of heredity: Stone's 27-year-old son, Sean, announced to the world, from Iran [where he had spent some considerable time among madman Ahmadinejad and assorted mullahs], that he had converted to Islam and that he now was "a Christian-Jewish Muslim." My first responsive thought was that, this was so surreal, it likely could end up as a potential film topic for young Stone's father, who like his son, would no doubt mold it into a sympathetic portrait of Iran's extremely theocratic regime.)

"... The fiction of top-down Government Control, of a Command Economy, is, at essence, like a Reality Show, which is to say a fraud." That statement, early in David Mamet's 2011 book, *The Secret Knowledge: On the Dismantling of American Culture*, captures *his* essence as a born-again conservative and genuine patriot who has at last seen the light. The fraud Mamet refers to exists because, unlike the natural state of a free-market economy and a free society in general, such systems are forced and unnatural – something it took Mamet all these years to finally realize, and in the most sobering manner possible.

Mamet admits reaching his realization after reading Friedrich Hayek's *The Road to Serfdom*, regarding there being a cost to everything, especially freedom and genuine justice, as opposed to the contrived concept of so-called social justice. He says the term "social justice" was invented to correct an observed inequality among the masses. In a free environment, while it may be tough, it is correct that choices always must be made. As Mamet puts it, "The Government could only profess to do more, its bureaucrats and politicians playing on our human need for guidance and certainty, and, indeed, our desire for Justice."

Culture plays a key role in establishing *morés*, Mamet says, but it is not germane to the Left, which ignores traditional cultural influences. To liberal revisionists, societal elements are constantly at odds with cultural development. For example, such "good ideas" as birth control, "diversity," free love, feminism, "and other 'counter-cultural' innovations spawned in the 1960s." Three of the latest so-called innovations Mamet cites are "the grand visions of Urban Planning, which destroyed the Black Neighborhood, Welfare, which destroyed the Black Family, and Affirmative Action, which is destroying Black Youth."

This is all happening in rapid-fire succession, with Mamet surmising that "the millennia-long evolution of the human family as a means of dealing with the environment was discarded by my generation of fantasists, in favor of a concept not only artificial, but inchoate: 'Freedom' – the pursuit which has led to misery." The social costs, he elaborates, include "angry feminists, lonely aging males, full divorce courts, broken families, grieving children, and a growing disbelief not only in the possibility of domestic accord, but in the efficacy of the free market."

Something very obvious – and on which I agree strongly with Mamet completely -- is his basic contention that modern education, especially liberal arts curricula at the college level, rarely applies to actual work-life and adulthood. He discerns that school shootings like Columbine (which coincidentally happened in my old congressional district while I was in office, unfortunately) are a direct byproduct of "what is not taught" and a consequent confused society rife with non-accountability and aberrant behavior choices. "… Mastery of a fungible skill is unnecessary in contemporary society," Mamet states.

After mentioning that "our laws and our culture as a whole have conclusively *rejected* racism," Mamet expresses puzzlement about an obvious contradiction: "Why does it delight the Left to claim the contrary?" Which gets right to the heart of revisionism -- what leftists usually say is the exact opposite of the facts. Look no further than Barack Obama and those who share his core philosophy.

What I call the Hypocrisy of Hate is evident in Mamet's assessment that the envy of the world toward our free-market system often results in hatred and overstated vitriol. American leftists and their comrades "are here not because we are the Great Satan, but because they are free to speak … and when they write they copyright their books, and buy goods with the proceeds," he accurately reasons.

Inculcated by liberal beliefs throughout the education system, many of today's young people (or anybody under, say, 40) wind up in self-centered, self-contained communities surrounded by liberals and liberal orientations. Therefore, Mamet concludes, this product of a liberal arts education "will quite literally *never*, cradle-to-grave, encounter a conservative idea, let alone a conservative." It is a similar journey to that, no doubt, encountered by the late *New Yorker* magazine film critic Pauline Kael after Republican Richard Nixon massacred liberal Democrat George McGovern in the 1972 presidential election. With an apparently straight face, Kael commented, "I can't see how this happened. I don't know *anyone* who voted for Nixon." As Mamet puts it, contemporary youth have grown up in "a parallel country," where there are two cultures occupying the same space.

There are numerous words or phrases included in a glossary, cited by Mamet, of "those things which previous tradition or mere observation revered as absolute good," and therefore must be mocked. Among these are: Initiative, individualism or ambition: "Greed" to the revisionists; development: "exploitation"; defense: "war-mongering"; use: "exploitation" or "despoliation"; inevitable global conflicts: "nationalism"; laws sufficiently strict enough to provide actual behavioral guidelines: "injustice" ; spending: "investment"; and religion (except maybe Islam, of course): "superstition." Moreover, in my mind, religion has basically been replaced by diversity, social justice, environmentalism, humanitarianism and so forth.

Rather than the popular and fantasial mindset that communism was the reason there had been a secure Europe throughout the decades of the Cold War, Mamet posits that the Marshall Plan and security "created by American military strength and determination" were the generators of a free, thriving post-war continent.

Mamet asks: "Is it not time for a return to that revolutionary understanding" regarding public servants, who are granted, *by the public*, "only that freedom of action necessary to fulfill that oath" of swearing to defend and protect the Constitution. As a former elected official at more than one level who was able to preserve the spirit of this oath to the best of my ability, I can personally attest that this is the true sense of liberty. That is opposed to the contrarians' concept in a warped belief that the State should impose its will on the people, rather than the people *granting* the permission to act on their behalf, yet only in the most limited sense. This was evident in spades during the debt-limit debate in summer 2011 when the Left encouraged even more damaging taxation and spending on virtually worthless revisionist-thrust social and "feel-good" programs but openly cheered any proposed cuts in funding for genuinely effective and proven defense and security mechanisms. The underpinning of where our society has erred is a total departure from the founding principles, the whole of which liberal revisionists have turned on its head, often in a seditious and traitorous way – and always as loudly as they can do it. Their protestations are an example of the most-virulent and genuine "hate speech."

As our productive nation becomes a collection of less-productive "occupants" (legal or illegal) rather than industrious "resident" citizens, plunging further headlong into deeply embedded socialism, I am reminded of a favorite episode of the former longtime popular television situation comedy, *All in the Family*. One day, family patriarch Archie Bunker, a blue-collar workingman whom the Left loved to revile, is sitting in his familiar easy chair sifting through the daily mail when non-working, pot-smoking son-in-law Mike Stivic, a darling of liberals, dares to complain. Stivic, whom Archie refers to as "Meathead," inquires: "Hey, Arch, why don't I ever get anything in the mail?" Bunker seems to ignore him, declaring, as he sorts each piece, with the word, "resident," then suddenly blares: "Here, Meathead. Here's something for you – 'occupant'." In conjunction with the increasingly damaging rhetoric spewed by socialists to encourage the type of behavior of a character (double meaning intended) like Mike Stivic, Mamet describes the byproduct as "accepted by a drugged populace and a supine press." It is the engine that drives the societal decline. While that decline is disgusting, it is understood, since it began early in a child's existence as what the liberal-turned-conservative playwright terms "Pediatric Socialism."

I wonder if, like me, someone such as Mamet, while possibly conceding that there may be some validity to such diagnoses as Attention Deficit Disorder and Attention Deficit Hyperactive Disorder, questions the strong arm of the American Psychiatric Association in dosing so many children with medications like Ritalin. I pose this quandary only because, in my childhood, there always were "frisky" kids, who were made to stand in the corner or put in a dunce stool until they wised up; no drugs were used. Could it be that mass dispensing of drugs to combat "disorders" is yet another socialistic attempt to control the populace at an early age, and therefore revise tradition?

Our civilization, which is incapable of dealing with the natural, God-given phenomenon of rowdy young boys "through immemorial means (discipline, order, sport, parental punishment, the military), deems the behavior pathological and administers wholesale diagnoses, sanctions, and drugs," Mamet writes. It is easy to see why these diagnoses are commonplace. The American Psychological Association's policy-making board voted unanimously, 157-0, in August 2011 to support same-sex "marriage," according to LifeSiteNews.com. This marked the eighth consecutive year of rubber-stamping this deviant behavior, but, even more shocking, homosexuality was declassified as a mental disorder in 1973 in the *Diagnostic and Statistical Manual of Mental Disorders*, following years of lobbying by homosexual-rights groups. (It all seemed a precursor to the unfortunate wave of same-sex civil unions and "marriages" sanctioned by various judicial activists in black robes and far-left legislatures in 2013.)

Like me, Mamet finds an inherent contradiction in the constant revisionist demands for reparations and/or apologies for slavery, Japanese internment and Chinese "coolie" labor, for instance, but rhetorically asks: "Are the ancestors of the 300,000 white males who died to defeat slavery (in the Civil War) excepted from apology?

"How is it that, sixty-some years after the West defeated Nazi Racism, we are enmeshed in a race-based culture, and making governmental decisions on the basis of genetics?"

A fairly recent television commercial by a competitor of a major telecommunications company that acquired a similar utility in Colorado and 12 other states in 2011 focuses on the ability to have choice. The advertisement, which depicts two dark-suited men, who strangely and symbolically resemble stereotypical government bureaucrats, underscores what occurs when an individual loses the natural capability to choose, and his "choice" is dictated by the suits. I mention this because Mamet muses about just such a scenario:

> "We have abundant natural resources but if there were a system in which there was no waste, we would be wearing the same clothes, for our clothes would be chosen for us on the basis of the theory of maximum conservation of resources. As would our cars. But suppose someone wanted a different car. Could he alter it? With what resources, if the state decided he had 'all that he needed'?"

Then, Mamet continues, if the man's eventual invention were taken by the state – "appropriated for the good of all" (as in Ayn Rand's *Atlas Shrugged*) – it would be the epitome of the socialist vision which "constrains human inventiveness and imagination."

David Mamet is absolutely correct when he asserts that "liberalism is a Religion (or as radio talker Michael Savage and others insist, a mental disorder). Its tenets cannot be proved, its capacity for waste and destruction demonstrated. But if affords a feeling of spirit. Rectitude at little or no cost." Remember he stated early in his new book that there is a cost to *everything* – which is an alien idea to liberals, who only envision a cost to others when redistributing Other People's Money. You see, this is what it means when we insist that liberalism, or socialism, or whatever you want to call it, replaces tradition – with the ultimate result being the tearing down of that tradition with revisionism. There exists, in reality, on nearly every moral issue or dilemma, a certitude of black or white, or no real gray area. Mamet illustrates this by using "the Liberal attitude to our toward our war with radical Islam as an example:

> "American liberals do not wish to surrender *their* particular country, but many wish Israel to surrender hers; they wish to have someone else (the Israelis) pick up the cost of their own psychological upset."

The essence of socialism, then, in Mamet's view (and mine, and that of every genuine traditionalist), "is for Party A to get Party B to give something to Party C." So, in addition to desired redistribution, we see the added, ugly specter of anti-Semitism (as I suggested in the

Prologue regarding the Occupy movement). In today's politically correct society, "it is not the absence of government but the rejection of culture which leads to anarchy," Mamet says.

I know that Franklin D. Roosevelt, despite his definite socialistic leanings, was not an anarchist, but his administration, for whatever set of reasons, was the critical period when the stage was set for everything negative and anarchistic that has happened since then. The massive cultural transformation physically and emotionally started to accelerate in the '60s, with sex-education classes, Vietnam war protests and feminism. All these manifestations – which rejected traditional culture as we knew it -- were from the Left's favorite playbook, *The Communist Manifesto*, by Karl Marx and Friedrich Engels.

To liberals, according to Mamet, "Government is merely one of the ways in which humanity may be convened to order its various affairs ... but the *only* way ... for if government is not only good, but the only source, why should it not be elaborated and empowered to address any and all issues?

"This is the vision of FDR, who elaborated a bad economic downturn into the worst depression in history" and, therefore, dismantled the free market by overloading the country with irrevocable social programs. The Rooseveltian revolution of one "alphabet-soup" agency after another – from the NRA (National Recovery Administration, as opposed to the later, non-governmental

National Rifle Association) to the TVA to the WPA –
saddled us all with ongoing debt that has burgeoned to
today's multi-trillion-dollar levels, and left innumerable
social problems in its wake.

We have a choice today of an omnipotent
government having too much power or a free market in
which ideas naturally flow and greatness ensues. However,
Mamet says, because of revisionists and their zeal for
social justice, people too often fall prey to the fantasial
lure of the former. That is why it has become increasingly
easier for people in general to accept the idea of a world
government. "The Left longs for the one-party State or
dictatorship," which rather than unity is "slavery."

I wrote in a column in August 2011 for
WorldNetDaily that it is not enough merely to slow growth
of government. To save our republic and resuscitate the
economy, we need not slow down the growth of
government; we need to come to a full stop, then reverse
course.

Like Oliver Stone, actors, writers and other artists
wind up being dupes for dictators and totalitarian
propaganda, because, as Mamet reasons, they are "easily
manipulated ... by the unconscious appeal of a universe
resembling their own (in which they are the hero)."
Consequently, in my mind, all the trappings of the "New
Society" make the average, non-performing person
susceptible to the idyllic fantasy of socialism. "No
wonder, then," Mamet laments, "that (those) of my
particular racket, show business, have been trotting the

globe for a hundred years, petted by and championing the cause of tyrants." To wit: Jane Fonda, Sean Penn and countless others.

Although Stone is not mentioned by name in Mamet's book, he definitely is an exception when Mamet states that few directors are smitten by despots, such as two of Stone's aforementioned heroes, Cuba's Fidel Castro and Venezuela's late Hugo Chavez.

"Why?" Mamet asks. "A director cannot deal in fantasy. His job is to take the delineation of fantasy (a script) and transform it into film-in-the-can." Plus, as more of an entrepreneur than an actor, a director is exposed to "the genius of America, and the American system of Free Enterprise." I ask, then, what happened to Oliver Stone in that context?

Having witnessed the legislative and bureaucratic processes up close, firsthand, I can attest to the utter uselessness and socialistic bloat of the 40-plus unelected "czars" appointed by Barack Obama. Each of these – unscreened and unconfirmed by the Senate via advise-and-consent enshrined in the U.S. Constitution – is in addition to all of the various Cabinet secretaries. Mamet agrees with my discontent in this regard:

> "Contemporary Liberal sentiment endorses the abrogation or elaboration of law to ensure that *no one* suffers, but the first and most important task of law in a democracy is not to right individual wrongs, but to ensure that no

one suffers *because of the State*. And the simple, tragic truth is that this may be accomplished not by a Czar or a committee, or by reorganization, or by accession to office of the Benevolent or Wise, but only by limiting the State's power."

Liberal thinking, Mamet insists, embraces "the false," such as higher taxes meaning increased prosperity, and accepts "the moot," such as global warming, as incontrovertible. "All strife to the Left is error, and poverty and all human ills eradicable by new programs" – which also are "revolutionary revisions (that) destroy the human ability to interact, which, in its entirety, is known as Culture."

American language, as we have experienced in at least the past two decades, or more, "is now subject to revision by those screaming the loudest." In other words, one does not to have to have anything cogent, logical and moral to say to be heard; one only need to holler louder for change to be effected. This revision of basic, generally accepted conduct of many centuries standing results in "an atmosphere not of happy compliance, but of anxiety, circumlocution, and a formalism destructive of the free exchange of ideas."

The net effect of all this is a ravaging of a beautiful culture through an ongoing attempt to discard time-honored traditions by creating a *new* culture that is "confusing, amorphous, and constantly shifting," Mamet says. I have seen this personally over the years as a guest on television political forums, where liberal hosts would rather not talk to *any* conservative at all, but revel in the opportunity to stack, say, three leftists against a single righty whom they can try to pound upon verbally with merciless gusto. However, just as often I have watched that lone conservative (me, Ann Coulter, Laura Ingraham, Mark Levin, or anyone) hold his or her own, and wind up winning these "debates," with logic, reason and truth, provided, of course, the liberals do not scream them into submission, as is their wont.

Mamet likens global politics to individual families. "The sick family employs the mechanism of the Designated Criminal ... who is always the single individual who dares question his family's interests and motives," even if he/she is reasonable and correct. "It is no great leap to discern, in the Family of Nations, this same mechanism – denial and coalescence around a lie." Instead of a Designated Criminal, the United Nations, for instance, is adept at choosing a Designated Criminal State" – too often that is the most free, most charitable and most accomplished country in the history of the world, the United States of America. It is funny that, when I served as an elected federal representative of this same, sovereign nation – and one who practiced *and* preached this idea of sovereignty and honoring of all borders – I felt like the Designated Criminal, as identified by liberal revisionists. It was a label I proudly wore, yet I simultaneously felt ashamed of liberal fellow Americans (some in my own political party) who wanted nothing more than, first, a denigration, and, ultimately, a disintegration of everything we hold dear.

The motive that drives revisionists is the stark contrast between what a truly free society regards as law versus their substitute of "fairness," the latter an artificial system where well-gotten gains are ripe for confiscation and redistribution. Mamet understands this when he lays out the following: "A rampant and untrammeled glee, an unchecked ambition for gain is, in the individual, called miserliness; in the society which strips him of it, it is called socialism."

When free enterprise is eliminated, in the guise of getting rid of greed, with that elimination will be the disappearance of all freedoms, Mamet says. Again, this is a central point in the *The Communist Manifesto*, the guidepost book for revisionists that was written in the 19th century, and supplemented in the 20th century by Marxist Saul Alinsky's *Rules for Radicals*. In either case, an optimum theme always is some subset of redistribution, or "taking from those according to their ability, and giving to those according to their need," as Barack Obama and his cultural-revisionist minions have foisted upon the rest of us.

"What is Liberal Education?" Mamet asks, then answers his own question: "It has become an indoctrination in aggressive Identity Politics, a schooling, that is, in the practice of indictment, assault, exclusion, and contempt, all of which contradicts the statement of Universal Humanity upon which all its educational 'ideology' rests." The trouble is, as he correctly deduces, many of the most outspoken campus radicals "were and are the children of privilege," often inherited. Therefore, while they never have "learned to obey, command, construct, amend, or complete – to actively contribute to the society," they have learned to be shrill. Mamet rightly describes their behavior as "a *developmental disability*; they (are) being drugged with self-indulgence," which somehow translates to idealism that ultimately creates the next wave of revisionists and sloganeers. So, like generation after generation of welfare recipients, we wind up with a similar cycle of brain-dead cretins to whom government becomes their religion – much to the detriment of society as a whole, both for the present and future.

As he excoriates feminists for exhibiting the typical double standard of the Left, David Mamet declares: "Matrimony and monogamy have forever been linked with property and inheritance, the nuclear family, in the West, having been decided upon through trial and error as the most effective unit for both." This segues well with the tried and true, centuries-old practice of connecting private property rights to other solid traditions. So, you can see, like other liberals, boilerplate feminists (whom I call Feminazis) pick and choose their victims, to defend – such as various serious violators of women like Bill Clinton and the late Ted Kennedy, because those men otherwise fit their "hero" niche. The *Newsweek* magazine cover dust-up in August 2011, however, whereby an ultraliberal editor made then-GOP presidential candidate Michele Bachmann look like a wild-eyed maniac, seemed to be a momentary tipping point in the other direction; a spokeswoman for the National Organization for Women was so outraged that even she had to condemn the cover, despite Bachmann's orthodox conservatism, saying that a male politician never would be subjected to the same treatment. I can tell you, though, from my own personal experience, that, like my former U.S. House colleague from Minnesota, *I* have been the target of leftist "Photoshopping" when they wanted to make me look bad.

"The Right sees an erosion of marriage (evidenced by sex education, cohabitation, homosexuality, single motherhood, abortion), and understands it as a moral affront. But it is additionally, and perhaps, more basically, an attack on property," Mamet writes. It boils down to "destroy the family, and trust the State." In what he terms a "return to nature," Mamet decries that socialists revel in the vision of an omnipotent "State, from which all blessings flow, which never wanes but always waxes in power, which cannot be wrong (.)"

Mamet traces the onset of the difference between (genuine) "justice" and "social justice" back to the separation of Judaism among Ashkenazi immigrants from Europe. The German Jews, who arrived first, generally in the late 19th century, embraced the more amorphous Reform movement. The poorer, less-educated and less-erudite Polish Jews, conversely, either retained their Orthodox roots or morphed into Conservative Judaism, which was somewhere between the Reform and Orthodox sects. The Reform direction, Mamet explains, set the launching ground for such left-leaning manifestations as "SDS (the grossly misnamed Students for a Democratic Society), American Buddhism, est, the Hunger Project, MoveOn.org, various cults, and the Democratic Party."

Here's Mamet's very cogent interpretation of how "feelings," or therefore immoral judgment, have come greatly into play in our justice system, especially in that form dispensed by judicial activists, such as Obama-appointed U.S. Supreme Court justices Sonia Sotomayor and Elena Kagan (both fit the category of shrill voices from the left who dictate their perverse "morals" to the rest of us):

"This expression of 'sympathy,' as in the action of most of contemporary Big Government, is the usurpation by the elected (or appointed) of the rights of others. The judge who forgot the admonition in Proverbs, "Do not favor the rich, neither favor the poor, but do Justice,' who set aside the laws, or who 'interpreted' them in a way he considered 'more fair,' was, for all his good intentions, robbing the populace of an actual possession (the predictability of legal codes). He was graciously giving away something which was not his.

"Government programs of confiscation and redistribution are called the War on Poverty, or the New Deal, or Hope and Change," Mamet says, "but that these programs are given lofty names ensures neither that their intentions are lofty, nor that even, if so, they will or *could* lead to lofty results." Those untroubled by graft and corruption ultimately associated with government plans are termed "liberals" by Mamet. Everyone else "we know as Conservatives."

I have believed for a long time – and it is painfully obvious – that the core family unit is the foundation for the rest of society's building blocks. When this reality ceases to exist, young people turn to gangs and other miscreant behavior as a substitute, with the ultimate price being an ongoing further societal and cultural erosion. When I see such seemingly mundane, yet increasingly more-common, appearances as tattoos, body-piercing, backward ball caps and limp arms dangling from open car windows, I wonder if the individuals to whom they are attached might be missing a father-figure or healthy nuclear family, or what *exactly* went wrong for society to allow these baseless, banal, yet defiant, demonstrations of expression. David Mamet basically concurs, writing that "the effective organ for transmission of cultural information is the family."

Mamet says that "if the home is destroyed, or its influence negated or derided (as it was both by Welfare, and it is in today's Liberal Arts "education"), (the child) is hard-pressed to come, through the force of his own reason, to a practicable ethical view of the world."

As both Mamet and I had mentioned earlier in this chapter, FDR's New Deal programs were anathema to the free market and the whole idea of freedom in general. Government produces make-work jobs at taxpayer expense, but doles them out "less efficiently" than private enterprise, Mamet says. "A perfect example is the Civilian Conservation Corps in the New Deal, which, as Thomas

Sowell has pointed out, was merely giving twenty thousand shovels out to do the work which could be accomplished by fifty bulldozers. Why not then, as he suggested, enlarge the paradigm, replace the shovels with three million teaspoons?" The New Deal is cited as but one terrible idea that stifled free enterprise. "What's the one institution which will not suffer through confiscation and the abrogation of the rule of law?" Mamet asks, again providing the answer: "Government." Or Barack Obama's imagined vision of "shovel-ready" government – which the 44th President admitted later was a lie in its own right.

To illustrate the "essence" of Marxism, Mamet compares a skilled performer like a doctor to an unskilled street sweeper, and wonders: "How can Government raise the wages of the street sweeper? Only by taxing its citizenry, which is to say only by overriding the *societal* decision that the skilled worker is entitled to higher pay than the unskilled." We heard the Left's shrillness again in mid-2011, when unionized teachers illegally called in sick to wage loud, disruptive demonstrations in the rotunda of the Wisconsin State Capitol, protesting laws passed by the Republican majority state Senate that greatly diminished the collective-bargaining ability of taxpayer-funded public-sector unions.

Government is good at "stating inchoate goals ... when indicting those who question them as traitors or ogres." Witness the constant attacks of Tea Party protesters as "terrorists" by someone as highly placed as Vice President Joe Biden for dare exercising their right and people's mandate to demand stoppage of insane

spending by Congress and the Obama administration.
That righteous protesters raise their voices against
governmental excesses and true tyranny is justice in its
own right, as it provides a counter to the shrill Left.

There is an inherent contradiction among young
Liberal/Socialist/Radicals, something Mamet hits with
bulls-eye accuracy when he states: "Frightened of
choice, they band together, dress, speak, and act alike, take
refuge in the herd, and call it 'individualism'." Naturally,
nothing is attractive about this course of action. Therefore,
because it is indeed an ugly manifestation of human
behavior, its adherents find they must yell and scream –
often profanely – to get attention and purportedly to force
everyone else into a similar state of group-think.

Says Mamet, "Those we loved, 'the oppressed,'
were those whose consciousness we denigrated
sufficiently to presume they would believe our
pretensions." He cites as an example why "the Left prefers
the Arabs to the Israelis," and also why they obsess "over
our country being 'liked.'

"We have created a permanent underclass through
the ignorant and sententious opinions of the mis-educated
and ignorant."

Pondering the gullibility of the public to willingly
accept and conform to false diversity, Mamet declares :
"The great fault of my generation is not ingratitude but
incomprehension. *Someone* must make the money.
Someone must provide the goods and services we all

enjoy. ..." I personally saw this unfold in astounding fashion one day while listening to a news report sometime during the Obama presidency shortly after his first "stimulus" was announced. A Detroit television reporter was interviewing two black women on a Motor City street. The women were elated, amid a double-digit unemployment rate in their city, to each be receiving a $250 "gift" from the ever-benevolent government. The interviewer, trying to capitalize on their elation, asked the women where the $250 came from. "Obama," one replied. "Where did Obama get it?" the reporter inquired. "From his stash," the same woman responded, "Obama's stash."

I guess the bottom line, if I ever wanted to hire a director to make a movie about harsh reality rather than the typical Hollywood fantasy, is that my man would be David Mamet. Oliver Stone (and fellow liberal revisionist director Michael Moore, for that matter) would be on the outside looking in – no doubt covetously thinking how he might appropriate the film's proceeds and redistribute them to a third party, "according to need," as Karl Marx taught him.

HATING AMERICA

5

ED SCHULTZ AND THE MSNBC ANTI-PATRIOTS

"Americans don't want condescension and platitudes. We know a mistake when we see one. ... The president forgets that we don't work for *him*. He works for *us*. With the job comes accountability. All the American people want from this administration is a little reassurance. ..."

It sounds a lot like how disgusted Americans felt about Barack Obama, his failed policies, his total lack of accountability and his cavalier attitude toward the average taxpayer, does it not? Well, this passage, on the back of the dust jacket of his 2004 book, *Straight from the Heartland*, is what Ed Schultz had to say about George W. Bush, Dick Cheney and their presidential administration. Schultz is one of the assorted screamers at low-rated cable television network MSNBC, which has taken yelling, ultra-leftist radicalism and a real sense of anti-patriotic blather to a new apex. What is perhaps more perplexing to me about Schultz than his other liberal and socialist cohorts on their network is that he, as a self-styled former Republican, professes to be "different." However, when you parse through his pronouncements, you still find a steadfast lefty and supreme Obama defender.

Over the years, I have had my share of on-air shouting matches with Schultz and his MSNBC colleagues, who, on a daily basis, demonize me and those who dare think the way I do. MSNBC, of course, originated several years ago as a joint-venture of Microsoft and the left-leaning, Obama-coddling National Broadcasting Co., ostensibly to incorporate the cutting-edge of computer technology with the 24-hour news cycle. Instead, the project has morphed into a dangerous and anti-American collection of shouting liberals and socialists who revel not only in misstating and misrepresenting obvious facts, but also who indulge in constant character assassination. I may be unpopular at MSNBC, but it does no one any good when I get called a name like "Crank-Credo" simply because there is vehement disagreement with my viewpoint or philosophy. (Even one of the token MSNBC-type liberals at more-balanced Fox News Channel, open-borders advocate and general loose-wire Bob Beckel, revels in referring to me as "that kook Tancredo out of Colorado."). I guess so few viewers tune in to MSNBC that it prompted GQ magazine in November 2011 to dub Schultz No. 3 on the list of "The 25 Least Influential People Alive." Barack Obama BTW was selected No. 25. GQ reckoned, "Then there are pundits like Ed Schultz. Do you watch 'The Ed Show' on MSNBC? Of course you don't. No one does. The only reason people watch 'The Ed Show' is they are working out in a hotel gym and they can't find a staff member to change the channel to ESPN." Ditto, I say, because anytime I travel, I notice that television sets in restaurants or airports are invariably tuned either to MSNBC or CNN – for the exact reasons GQ cited.

Although he may not have intended to be so blatant, one of the ring-leaders, Lawrence O'Donnell, one night on his MSNBC show, declared: "Don't call me a liberal; I'm a socialist, and proud of it." It is that simple. O'Donnell was a script-writer/producer for the long-running NBC dramatic series, *The West Wing*, which ended an eight-year run in 2006. The scripts were imbued with all of the bias and vitriol toward conservatives that one would expect from O'Donnell, left-wing *West Wing* creator Aaron Sorkin and their lot. Plus, you must remember that when lefties cannot win with logic, they resort as an automatic default mechanism to name-calling and talking over debate opponents.

Moreover, part and parcel of the liberal/socialist *modus operandi* is the incredible double standard, wherein the mainstream media mavens and moguls have protected Barack Obama or other kinsmen, but jump at moment's notice to criticize someone such as the 2012 GOP presidential hopefuls or Sarah Palin. Former presidential candidate Herman Cain had been set aside for special bad-mouthing, since having a black conservative male in national politics dispels the liberal myth of where blacks automatically owe their allegiance. Cain, contrary to this stereotype, actually came across during Republican presidential debates in which he participated as perhaps the most authentic person on the stage, despite attacks leveled at him for alleged sexual escapades. It is indeed unfortunate that unproven allegations ultimately caused Cain to suspend his campaign.

In May 2011, I faced my own "inquisition" at the hands of Martin Bashir, an MSNBC host of Indian descent who is a native of Great Britain. Bashir earned his broadcasting spurs long before his MSNBC employment with a series of interviews and investigative reports he did when the late Michael Jackson was accused of sexually abusing children. Bashir ambushed me by using one of my columns to ask me if I wanted President Obama killed after our brave U.S. Navy SEALS had slain Osama bin Laden. Actually, I had written that Obama was a more serious threat to America than al-Qaeda. My rationale, I had written, was that we know that Bin Laden and followers want to kill us, but at least they are an outside force against whom we can offer our best defense. By contrast, we are almost defenseless against Obama and his lackeys, but we squandered the only way to remedy that in 2012 -- to take them out IN AN ELECTION.

"Wasn't that a ludicrous thing to accuse the president of?" Bashir asked, as if he were Torquemada and I were a 15th-century religious apostate. I fired right back and told Bashir it was ludicrous on his part to make such an analogy and I further said I was pleased about Bin Laden's killing. As we proceeded, Bashir asked, "To follow your logic, would you have preferred then the death of the president, as opposed to Bin Laden?" I replied: "No, of course not. My God. And that is not a logical assumption anybody can make." Then after Bashir pointed out my statement about Obama being a greater threat "than Osama bin Laden (I had said "al-Qaeda"), I tried, probably in vain, to insist that I didn't want any violence or harm to come to Obama, "except political harm" (again at the ballot box).

What I experienced with Martin Bashir is a daily occurrence on MSNBC, whether the "host" is Bashir, O'Donnell, Rachel Maddow, Chris Matthews, Chris Hayes, Schultz or whomever. Character assassination always comes first, while facts and logic are relegated to the back seat. (The only "conservative" concessions on the network have been my old friend, the indefatigable Pat Buchanan, and my former GOP congressional colleague Joe Scarborough, the latter really having left the reservation long ago, if ever he was a true conservative. However, the intolerant management at MSNBC in January 2012 indefinitely suspended Buchanan, largely because, it is widely believed, of a controversial new book he had just released, then they summarily "exiled" him forever a month later, permitting him to move more appropriately to fair-minded Fox News as a regular contributor. So much for tolerance of opposing viewpoints at MSNBC, right?)

Schultz, whom top radio talker (and frequent Schultz target) Rush Limbaugh always calls "Sergeant Schultz," for his perceived similarity to the bumbling Nazi non-com of the old *Hogan's Heroes* TV series, is a classic example of one's mouth moving before the brain can catch up. The anchor of the former weeknight "The Ed Show" (banished in March 2013 to weekends-only) claims, of course, to be a former conservative who had a Damascus Road-like conversion to liberalism years ago after a "date" with his wife-to-be at a Salvation Army shelter she ran in his old broadcasting beachhead of Fargo, N. Dak.

Schultz was suspended for a week without pay in May 2011 (coincidentally in the same month as my dust-up with Bashir) after he called another conservative radio talk-show host, Laura Ingraham, a "right-wing slut." Within a day, Schultz was forced to issue an on-air apology, dripping with false remorse. According to the "On Media" report of the online website *Politico*, Schultz's temper has reportedly gotten him in trouble before. *Page Six* (of the *New York Post*) reported ... that he threatened to 'torch this (bleep)ing place' after MSNBC failed to include him in election-night promos. Sources said that MSNBC brass threatened to fire him if he repeated the outburst, though MSNBC declined to comment on it at the time. A month later, *TV Newser* reported that he was reprimanded by MSNBC brass for calling New Jersey Gov. Chris Christie a 'cold-hearted fat slob.' "

One gets a window into Schultz's way of thinking in books he has authored. The aforementioned 2004 volume, *Straight from the Heartland*, which is subtitled *Tough Talk, Common Sense, and Hope from a Former Conservative*, was followed by another Schultz book, published in 2010, titled *Killer Politics*.

In much of the first book, Schultz outlines what he terms "The Four Pillars of a Great Nation: Defending America, A Sound Economy, Feeding the Nation, and

Educating America." While sounding good on the surface, the bromides contained in his "Pillars" are nothing more than a re-hash of the liberalism he has belatedly adopted. (He reiterates an updated version of the Pillars in his second book.)

But before he covers his Pillars in more depth, Schulz introduces readers to his journey, as to whom he has become and how he reached his philosophical junction, as ill-advised as that turn in his life was, in my estimation.

Schultz shows the inherent dishonesty that is rampant on the Left when he writes, "For the sake of this country and the First Amendment, balance must be restored to the airwaves." Who is he kidding? The Left has a lock-hold on the "Lamestream Media": The three major TV broadcast networks, *The New York Times*, *The Washington Post*, *Time* and *Newsweek* magazines, The Associated Press wire service, CNN, MSNBC, National Public Radio and most of academia. If it were not for Fox News Channel and the explosion of the New Media on the Internet, talk radio and in the Blogosphere, the kind of blather produced by Schultz and Co. would go totally unchecked.

If you do not believe a double standard exists in Liberal Land regarding the Bush and Obama administrations, then listen to this tidbit from Schultz's 2004 *Heartland* book: "My wife ... is a psychiatric nurse. When we sit around ... watching the talking heads on cable TV, I ask her to point out the really crazy ones. She nudges me when Cheney appears on the screen. We're still trying to get his medical records, but they're probably locked up in Rush's house." Schultz dares imply all this when it is liberals who steadfastly defend Barack Obama's "right" not to disclose similar information about himself, including medical, academic and birth records. Moreover, Schultz hints here at a conspiracy at the same time leftists constantly conspire to stonewall. It is hypocrisy run rampant.

It actually gets worse, as far as Schultz is concerned. "Apparently, dodging accountability is *modus operandi* in the White House," he writes of George W. Bush, perhaps not forecasting that these words would come back to haunt him and others of the Left many times over with Barack Hussein Obama.

One thing that is clear throughout the inaptly named *Straight Talk* is that Schultz, much like others of the self-described "progressive" label, chooses to attack opponents based on physical characteristics, perceived personality flaws or other superficial aspects rather than issues. This echoes the environment I have experienced time and again when I debate almost any lefty, plus the personal attacks always are accompanied by the incessantly loud volume of one talking over any attempts at logic or truly solving issues.

In addition to the usual misrepresentation of facts in which liberals indulge, Schultz brought forth during the early stages of the Iraq War "bogeymen," or "straw" figures, such as the following scenario, which never materialized:

> "Quietly, Selective Service has been gearing up to implement a draft within seventy-five days of the order. Bush won't tell you because it would kill any chance for re-election (in 2004)."

No, even the threat of re-institution of the military draft did not become close to reality until proposed by a liberal Democrat, New York's Charles Rangel, a discredited politician who several years later was censured by the U.S. House of Representatives for repeated shady financial dealings, then re-elected anyway in 2012.

In discussing the Iraq War in his book, Schultz uses his platform to disparage Bush, Cheney, Don Rumsfeld, and other Republicans, with an especially certain paranoia directed toward "neocons." This discussion is done in the context of Schultz's First Pillar: Defending America. Yet, other than the many cheap, partisan shots he levels, the Dakota talker offers few, if any, solutions – all typical for a revisionist.

The half-dozen "solutions" Schultz posits – border security, intelligence, accountability, regaining the trust of the military, and global strategy – are nothing more than lip-service and bromides straight out of the Democrat playbook. They include the usual calls for "proper" or "full" funding (whatever those terms mean, as long as beleaguered taxpayers foot the bill), alternative fuels and the oldie-but-baddie, "human rights."

Like other liberals and radicals already mentioned in this book, Schultz demonstrates economic illiteracy. He shows little grasp of the problems and resultant potential solutions in his Second Pillar: A Sound Economy.

As a true socialist would, Schultz lambastes the "wealthy" and decries a perceived severe "imbalance" between the haves and have-nots, advocating that the United States go down the same path as supposedly benign European nations, which "aren't afraid to tax the rich and provide more social programs for the poor and middle class," he laments.

"In these largely peaceful countries, health care is a right, not a privilege. In our country, corrupt alliances between Big Business and government (like Obama's crony capitalism, maybe, I wonder?) have created a stronghold on power," Schultz writes. "This unholy alliance has left the common man unprotected, as outsourced jobs continue to kill American families." Most of these other countries to which he refers have driven themselves over a financial cliff precisely because of the practices Ed Schultz advocates – to wit: Spaniards dumping their failed, seven-year experiment with socialism in late 2011. Does someone like Schultz possess the intellectual honesty to admit that when American companies outsource jobs, it is a direct response to overt taxation, forced unionism and other failed policies of tax-and-spend liberals in both parties? I doubt it.

Overregulation and the choking grip of neo-Marxist environmental groups also contribute to the exodus. In addition, the Prairie Blowhard either is ignorant of the Founders' intent or consciously chooses to admit that something such as health care is *not* a God-given right.

While Schultz was correct at the time about Enron, and companies like it, not being honest with ratepayers, especially in California, he is wrong to pin total blame for the collapse of the most-populous state's economy on that alone. What leftists conveniently forget is that the real set of reasons for California sinking into the sewer – economically, morally, every which way – is because of the ongoing, and increasing, grip of liberal special-interest lobbies, such as illegal-immigration advocates and their unbridled embrace of open borders, homosexuals, unions, trial lawyers and any other number of tax-and-spend forces. Couple with this the strangling hand of the federal government – for example, the Environmental Protection Agency and its "protection" of a small fish species that effectively helped create an unemployment rate of up to 50 percent in one of the nation's major breadbaskets, the San Joaquin Valley. (I will elaborate further on the specific excesses of the EPA and the Obama administration in general, and will take an updated look at California through the eyes of a trained resident-observer in later chapters.)

I talked extensively about economic illiteracy in the Prologue. Well, based on his Second Pillar "solutions," Ed Schultz proves that not only Occupy movement fleabaggers are not alone in cornering the market on economic illiteracy. Schultz professes a strong, and inherently bogus, belief in a worldwide minimum wage, "which," he insists, "would serve the dual purpose of lifting the standard of living for workers in Third World countries while allowing American products to be more competitive. It would slow the flow of jobs out of America." Sure, Ed, and the Wizard of Oz was not just a flim-flam man behind a curtain. Guaranteeing outcomes by artificially manipulating the economy never has worked; only free, unfettered markets, without unions or unnecessarily bloated minimum wages, do the trick in the long term. Once-useful unions long ago morphed into useless, self-promoting organizations that protect and promulgate mediocrity while ignoring merit and embracing largely communistic practices.

As for health care, in conjunction with his Second Pillar, Schultz stands foursquare behind mandated single-payer, universal coverage – something that is totally unconstitutional. So he must have rejoiced when Schultz's president-of-choice shoved Obamacare down our collective throats, helping congressional Republicans win in a landslide in 2010. As the citizenry continued to be beset with other take-it-or-leave-it propositions and were facing still-high gas prices and unemployment rates, poll numbers in 2012 offered clear evidence of the public's displeasure, yet despite that sentiment, Obama managed to win four more years.

In economic solutions related to his Second Pillar, Schultz addresses big-business corruption, outsourcing, the perceived wealth gap and health care. Trouble is, his recommendations are rife with the false egalitarianism, "justice," predictable advocacy of labor unions and shopworn governmental solutions for everything in which radicals revel. In most cases, these proposals are counter to our Founders' principles.

Whether through non-government-run homeless shelters, church-sponsored charities or the simple, voluntary largesse of private citizens' compassion, it is fitting that no one in this country starve to death. Of course, as Ronald Reagan always preached, there are the truly needy and, for them, there exists a limited role for government to lend a hand – but to do so only temporarily by casting a "safety net." This means there should not be generation-after-generation of "welfare families," composed of laggards simply unwilling to work or contribute meaningfully to society. It is not the taxpayers' responsibility to involuntary bear the burden of propping up these louts.

Converse to this thought, though, and predictably, is the Ed Schultz Third Pillar: Feeding the Nation.

As Schultz proceeds into his Third Pillar, with few exceptions his sources to support his contentions consist of either North Dakota's two Democrat senators at the time, both since-retired, Byron Dorgan and Kent Conrad; the socialistic Economic Policy Institute; the left-leaning National Farmers Union and Rocky Mountain Farmers Union; majority staff of Democrat-controlled Senate committees; and others with such a slant on food and nutrition issues that their left arms are close to falling off. Nowhere will you find a statistical buttressing from the more moderate American Farm Bureau Federation or its various state affiliates, so as to provide balance, despite Schultz's quite hollow plea that "we need more balance."

Just to prove further what a warped sense of proportion and values radicals like Schultz have, he offered evidence on a "trade mission" to Castro's Cuba in 2002 with state delegates from Minnesota and North Dakota. He was the only American broadcaster to do a live show from Havana, despite the ongoing U.S. trade embargo against this communist stronghold. My tears certainly were of the crocodile variety after reading the Prairie Blowhard's poignant plea to cut poor butcher Fidel Castro some slack:

> "Even after enduring forty years of isolation, Castro has managed to provide free medical care and college education to his people. The time has come to open the doors of commerce to Cuba. Castro is no saint, but I'm not sure he deserves a seat at the Axis of Evil table, either."

The supposed free health care certainly is offered to keep alive (as opposed to jailing or executing political dissidents) Castro's acolyte population of useful idiots long enough to continue to be educated (brainwashed, actually) in the finer points of Marxism. Because of any human being's natural yearning for freedom, the courageous ones – including many accomplished athletes – have defected to America and other free countries over the years, often at the cost of leaving behind family members. The yearning for liberty tends to become accelerated.

As with his other Pillars, Schultz presents several solutions in the Fourth Pillar: Feeding the Nation. The four major areas include food conglomerates, food policy, organization and starvation. Yet, similar to every other problem, he assigns tired, trite liberal antidotes. For instance, he advocates anti-trust legislation to break up otherwise legally existing food conglomerates, conceding, though, that "it is hard to say when exactly a company has crossed the line from competition to predation" -- if *ever* that happens with the frequency that Schultz imagines. While Schultz has no real solution for "organization," he suggests some form of cooperative, but to do so he falls back on the governmental idea of state agriculture departments "funding the venture until it could stand on its (own) feet," with involuntarily confiscated taxpayer money, of course. Even regarding his last recommendation, to stem starvation (despite a rare admirable idea that churches and other non-governmental organizations continue to do what they already accomplish), Schultz feels obligated to strongly encourage the dubious and criminal United Nations to lead such an effort.

In his Fourth Pillar: Educating America, Schultz quickly and unfortunately dismisses vouchers for private schools. "Shifting dollars from public education to private not only diminishes public education, it circumvents the line between church and state by giving federal funds to faith-based schools," he claims. No matter that plenty of parents – or taxpayers who have no school children – whose children do not attend public schools still pay taxes in the public school districts in which they reside. Leftists insist public schools have done such a great job over the years that vouchers and tuition tax credits are unnecessary –a fallacious argument if ever there was one, since public schools have increasingly become union-run factories that manufacture political correctness. Trust me; I am a former public-school teacher who has personally witnessed this folly.

Bear in mind, when our public schools continue to beg for more money, yet show less-than-noteworthy results, that "full funding" (as the big spenders insist upon) is actually a sophisticated money-laundering operation whereby involuntarily confiscated Other People's Money is collected "for the children." This is in addition to mandated dues paid by teacher/members to unions, then finally channeled back to the Democrat Party in the form of campaign contributions for compliant candidates, most of whom naturally *are* Democrats.

Schultz's four remedies for educating America are public schools, teacher pay, college and what he terms "cutting through the media clutter." The federal government, in the form of the utterly useless Department of Education for which I once was a regional director (actually, against my will but in service to my country when asked by President Reagan), is Schultz's first choice to take the lead, so as to guarantee outcomes. Ditto for boosting teacher pay, although in the previous paragraph I detailed what that actually means. Schultz has no real solution for the college conundrum, other than John Kerry's non-starting "tax-credit" plan that would have relied on $13 billion collected by the feds to continue to run the student-loan program, rather than it be administered privately as it had been for many years previously. Regarding the "media clutter" suggestion, Schultz does not really believe it in his heart when that would be counter to liberal orthodoxy. He encourages young people to glean information from varied sources, but again I question how heartfelt that sentiment is, considering the man making such a recommendation.

Ed Schultz's *Killer Politics* was published in 2010 and, instead of having the Bush administration to bash anymore, he was quick to employ the typical liberal double standard when assessing a Democrat president. After all, his man Barack Obama obviously has been a horseman riding astride a saddle on an oblivious journey into a New Apocalypse, dragging unwilling Americans kicking and screaming along the ground behind him. In the later book, Schultz already has jiggered the names of his Pillars, slightly re-naming them: Defend the Nation, Establish a Sound Fiscal Policy, Feed the Country, and Educate the People.

One constant throughout the 2010 work, just as was the case in Schultz's debut book, is that he is hypocritical and inconsistent in presenting viewpoints. Instead of staking himself with bedrock positions, he vacillates by seeming to stand foursquare behind a pronouncement, then within two or three paragraphs afterward, he contradicts himself. As for me, you can disagree with what I say – and you might, in some isolated cases, prove me wrong – but I am proud to have a firm set of values, rooted in decency, morality and constitutional principles, from which I will *never* waver. Can one honestly say the same about Ed Schultz and virtually anyone else on the Left? I think not.

Conceding that capitalism *does* work, Schultz proceeds to add: "With rules in place," his idea really being rules that should preemptively constrain market forces. He clarifies that capitalism only is feasible mixed with socialism, "in the right measure." (Is this man capable of taking a firm stand without any qualification or equivocation?) The fact is the free market needs to be allowed to operate totally *freely*, with a judicial system in place to offer legitimate redress to anyone who warrants it; such strangleholds as *faux*-environmental regulations, costly phony lawsuits and Obama's crony capitalism (all of in which he has favored his biggest campaign contributors) are roadblocks to commerce designed to keep power in the hands of the few selected special-interest groups.

Schultz again gets it backwards when he points to Obama's so-called Stimulus program for giving the country "confidence" that was "critical to stabilizing the economy" and terms the Cash for Clunkers scheme "a shot in the arm to automakers and their suppliers." What?!

Then, why did the real, adjusted unemployment rate continue to hover in or near double digits and the deficit and national debt keep ballooning to record highs over the past four years? Barack Obama *did* inject "confidence" into our economy, only the definition is different – sort of like the confidence of convicted conman Bernie Madoff.

Ed Schultz naturally lays the blame for all this "excruciatingly slow process" at the feet of "Republican obstructionists in the Senate who drag out each bill and amendment." That is funny to me since, during the entire Obama presidency, the Democrats and Majority Leader Harry Reid controlled what I sometimes call "the world's most-boring deliberative body." Obama and the senators in the majority party assumed no blame whatsoever, yet they were quick to take credit for anything perceived as positive (translation: Picking public pockets again).

"The less we depend on the rest of the world for energy, or *anything*, for that matter, the less pressure we put on our military," Schultz writes. While this is true on its face, the trouble is he wrongly believes that such *supplemental* alternative energy sources as solar and wind can replace oil. The real key to solving our basic energy problems long-term is tapping all available domestic sources, be they via the resurgence of drilling (whether offshore or in the newly discovered, massive Bakken fields in northwestern North Dakota), building new refineries, mining clean coal, tapping vast natural-gas reserves all over the West through hydraulic fracturing ("fracking") and taking advantage of the prolific oil sands in the Canadian province of Alberta. The Obama administration, dominated by Marxist environmentalists – both from within and outside "green" activists – initially announced in November 2011 that it was delaying any decision on the proposed, $7 billion Keystone XL pipeline to placate environmentalists. Then in January 2012, the president further declared that Keystone would be delayed at least until 2013, after the 2012 presidential election. Even though it would take several years for build-out, once the 1,700-mile pipeline from Canada to Texas is completed, it could go a long way in reducing dependence on foreign oil and directly providing as many as 20,000 jobs -- and indirectly lead to thousands more -- but when radical green zealots scream, the Obamatrons have dutifully listened.

In his own version of trying to change history – perhaps through omission as well as changing facts – Ed Schultz lambastes George W. Bush for lack of intelligence communications between the CIA and FBI as the cause of the 9-11 attacks. Schultz conveniently forgets that it was Deputy Attorney General Jamie Gorelick, DURING THE CLINTON ADMINISTRATION, who created the "wall" between the two agencies. What is scary still is that the Obama Justice Department has relied on Gorelick's advice and obviously poor and perilous judgment. So when will the next terrorist attack be, in light of this, and in what form will it be – chemical, biological, radiological – and will lack of border security precipitate it?

Calling for more "fairness" in trade agreements, Schultz really means unionizing the whole world – which, of course, would bloat prices to unrealistic levels. To do this, he reasons, we must "massage unfair trade agreements so that they become 'more fair.'" This, in Schultz's mind, would involve "cutting some Third World countries a little slack in trade deals to help lift them up." What I say is that we reinstitute strictly free-market principles in trading with *everyone,* letting those market forces naturally dictate who become winners and losers, not create an expansion of U.S.-funded welfare policies to the rest of the world.

Schultz is especially fond of the union-pushed Employee Free Choice Act, which, like almost any left-wing proposal, does exactly the opposite of its title. If it became law, the act would allow unions to dictate to businesses a rigged agenda, rather than "strengthen the bargaining power of all workers," as Schultz and its proponents profess.

"Where would we be without unions?" he asks. Any good that unions accomplished occurred decades ago; it has been a long, long time since unions worked in favor of the public good. Unions have become so anathema to most Americans, in fact, that fewer than 12 percent of all American workers today belong to a union and, among those, only one in seven belongs to a private-sector union; the rest are members of public-employee unions whose involuntarily collected (coerced?) dues are a funding mechanism for Democrat candidates through an ongoing "laundering" process.

Someone like Ed Schultz, albeit a professed long-ago former Republican himself, never will give a Republican, *any* Republican, much credit for anything positive. For example, his perception of mid-1990s reforms was that President Clinton did it all on his own -- a sure sign of historical myopia. Had it not been for a majority-GOP Congress and its leaders' ability to convince Clinton to triangulate his inherent liberalism, there never would have been welfare reform or a concerted effort to achieve a balanced budget. Schultz's current perception (or more accurately, misperception) of Clinton's fellow Democrat, Obama, has taken a similar tack in assigning blame to the opposition when something has gone awry, yet predictably placing all praise, deserved or not, in Obama's bailiwick.

As he has in his first book, Schultz swears in *Killer Politics* that he has solutions to educate our young, yet he places his hope again in government. The panacea he produces includes total reliance on public schools (which, of course, are controlled lock-stock-and-barrel by the teachers' unions and the rest of the liberal education establishment of bureaucrats and school-board members) and a lot of other central-planning mechanisms "that allows people from all social strata to succeed." Translation: Guaranteed outcomes, no accountability and total egalitarianism – all at taxpayer expense. Because of students' general lack of enthusiasm, it "suggests that there is something terribly wrong with the way we are teaching our kids." Yes, indeed, what is wrong in the classroom is too much political correctness, sex education, bilingual education, ethnic studies and everything except the basics. "Not every teacher is competent or worth defending," Schultz declares in one breath, then reiterates his support of mediocrity-promoting teacher unions in the next in his classic contradictory fashion.

Demonstrating an awkward backward grasp of how ideology plays out in classrooms, he states that textbooks have been "more concerned with the political correctness of the day than with objective facts." Schultz's perception and definition of P.C. differ from mine, for he lays the blame at the feet of "a conservative group of shrill Christian fundamentalists." Truth be known, the majority of textbooks these days are contrarily politically correct in more of a left-leaning way, as the *theory* of evolution and man-made global warming/climate change are unabashedly presented as irreplaceable Gospel truth. "The politicization of the classroom reached a ridiculous high when President Obama sought to address America's students in 2009," Schultz says, adding that "the political blowback from the right wingers was so intense that many schools chose not to allow students to hear Obama's remarks, to avoid controversy." It is as if he gives no credit to the prudence of administrators or teachers for preemptively sniffing out a blatantly political speech by the Campaigner-in-Chief that would have been short on education but long on propaganda.

Schultz essentially unmasks himself as a prototypical radical, telling us, "the right thing to do is to make education a civil right just like health care," not just vague rights (neither of which, by the way, has ever been enshrined in the founding documents as *civil* rights).

"... We need to examine our role as an arms dealer to world," Schultz writes as a lamentation. Yes, especially in the Obama Justice Department, over which Eric Holder, the most dangerous attorney general in our nation's history, presided over the "Fast and Furious" gun-running scandal, belatedly and quite disingenuously disavowing knowledge of this distasteful and murderous program. Through the Bureau of Alcohol, Tobacco, Firearms and Explosives, an arm of the Justice Department, thousands of weapons were sold on the illegal-firearms market, winding up in the hands of Mexican drug cartels, whose henchmen the agency was trying to entrap executed hundreds of victims, including U.S. Border Patrol agent Brian Terry. Yet Eric Holder professed total ignorance of this deadly folly, and, as has always been the case on virtually any issue involving the Obamaites, received cover from the cadre of on-air Marxists at MSNBC and the big television networks along with the myriad sympathetic major print-media outlets.

The dishonesty of thought persists when Schultz attempts to make a case for Obamacare, the ham-handed effort to take over fully one-sixth of the nation's economy and handcuff Americans with single-payer, universal health care. He cites surveys that "showed a majority of Americans favored a government-run option to compete with private insurers." In actuality, opinion poll after opinion poll categorically has indicated that Americans soundly reject such a premise. So many Republican governors are doing all they can to reject the costly federal mandate of Obamacare, exercising their 10th Amendment right of states' sovereignty.

The Prairie Blowhard also calls George W. Bush "and his cronies" hypocrites "for effectively stalling stem cell research advances." I have mentioned my differences with Bush in other chapters of this book. However, I must emphasize that the 43rd president opposed public funding of *embryonic* stem cell research – for moral reasons; he was not opposed to privately funded *adult* stem cell research. In terming national health care "the smart money solution" Schultz and his cohorts are delusional in their belief that socialized medicine will not stymie private investment in research, and the same is true on the environment.

"According to the Sierra Club, power plant pollution is responsible for thirty thousand deaths each year," Schultz proclaims, using as his source one of the least-credible groups, one that *knows* it is peddling environmental folly in order to advance the collective power grab that has nothing really to do with pollution or the environment. "Additionally," he goes on, "power plants release over 40 percent of total U.S. carbon dioxide emissions, a prime contributor to climate change. … Scientists tell us if we do not begin reducing greenhouse gases now, climate change has the potential to dramatically and negatively change the way we live, to the point of planet-wide catastrophe. … All things considered, the evidence is overwhelming that mankind's actions have had a great effect on climate change and that we need to act quickly," Schultz says. "When you look at the corresponding rise of greenhouse gases and global temperatures, it's hard to argue. You certainly can't deny that our ice caps are melting." Schultz's main source of support and background is the ultra-leftist Union of Concerned Scientists.

Schultz actually believes that the Obama Cash for Clunkers program and Cap and Trade proposal contributed to solving pollution problems, yet they were nothing more than window-dressing wherein the taxpayer unwittingly funded new bureaucracies that did nothing more than pad the pockets of the president's own corporate cronies and added new public-sector union members. Ask yourself: If these programs were any kind of stimulant, then why did the unemployment rate under Obama continue to linger at just under 10 percent (and never get lower than 7.6 percent), as the administration used shady accounting tricks to "cook the books" in each monthly report?

Schultz is wrong because you *can* deny all this rot. There are many *real* scientists who vehemently disagree with this *faux*-science, and those genuine practitioners concede – as do average laymen like me – that, while there is a relatively negligible amount of man-made pollution, any actual "climate change" is miniscule and the result of naturally occurring meteorological phenomena. Those who share my view realize that taxpayer dollars should never be involuntarily confiscated by avowed Marxists hell-bent on controlling every aspect of our daily lives. Even worse is the disingenuousness of their designs; if they really were truthful, they never, ever, would be elected – except in only the most-gerrymandered and left-leaning legislative or congressional districts.

One of the main reasons the Left cannot govern the rest of us is their inherent misunderstanding of government's true role, a sentiment encapsulized in the following statement by Schultz (which indicates gross ignorance of the border security issue):

> "The primary reason for existence of the government is to pool resources so we can collectively do what we cannot achieve individually. You have to know where the people are so you can properly allocate resources. But when it comes to illegal aliens, we don't know as much as we should."

Actually, we know plenty. We know that illegal aliens drain our economy, our health resources and our social services system. We know that the main reason illegals pour into our country is an alarming lack of border security. We know that, for whatever reason it suits the needs of the open-borders crowd, the number of illegal aliens in the United States is greatly understated; while the actual number may approach 20 million-plus, the estimate always stated is typically somewhere between 10 million and 12 million.

Although I am not an elected official anymore, I feel it is my solemn duty to maintain leadership on an issue for which I am proud to have been the leading light for the decade I served in Congress. Part of this leadership mantle includes calling to public attention misinformation that is disseminated, especially in light of the 2013 proposed Senate Gang of Eight "comprehensive immigration reform" and The Associated Press decision to remove the term "illegal immigrants" from its stylebook. (BTW I suggested, echoed by comedian Jay Leno, that we simply now refer to illegal aliens as "undocumented Democrats" since that party is where the votes of these newly minted and "amnestized" hordes are likely to be cast.

Some selected instances of misinformation worth mentioning include:

> -- In a Republican presidential debate in November 2011, former U.S. House Speaker and GOP presidential candidate Newt Gingrich was incorrect in saying "Red Cards" he proposed were not a form of amnesty. Later the same week in my regular "Border Battlelines" column for *World Net Daily*, I corrected Gingrich and laid out how the so-called Red Card Solution is nothing more than another form of amnesty for illegals.

> -- In a November 2011 television debate I had with Colorado-based open-borders advocate Julien Ross (no relation to my collaborator on this book), he incorrectly stated that there already was 700 miles of fencing along the U.S.-Mexican border. In fact, I corrected him,

there has been only 23 miles constructed by the U.S.government on a border of about 2,000 miles. (Julien Ross must have read Ed Schultz's *Killer Politics* because the figures cited were exactly the same as Schultz's – both likely from the same talking points issued by open-borders, pro-illegal-immigrant advocates.)

-- In his *Killer Politics* book, Ed Schultz claims that illegal workers contribute to the economy because the Social Security Administration reported a net gain of $12 billion in 2007 from "undocumented workers." How is this possible with use of illegal, bogus Social Security numbers? There is a valid reason why they are "undocumented," since they lack valid documents, including legitimate Social Security cards. There is a crying need for a mandatory employment verification program called E-Verify, which would ensure employers are hiring people with legitimate birth and Social Security records. (As has been well-researched and documented by almost everyone except the mainstream media, even Barack Obama's birth "records" and Social Security number are highly suspicious. Therefore, does that make *him* an illegal alien until proved otherwise, thus rendering him constitutionally ineligible for office?)

-- I squared off in another TV debate in May 2011 with open-borders supporters Tamar Jacoby and San Antonio (Tex.) Mayor Julian Castro opposing me and current Kansas Secretary of State Kris Kobach, author of Senate Bill 1070, the Arizona immigration law. One of the things I emphasized during the forum was something I have been steadfast about regarding immigrants to this country – learning English. Moreover, I have advocated English as the country's official language, rather than the needlessness and exhaustive cost of printing ballots and other documents in more than 100 languages. I mentioned during the debate my genesis for this was, as the kid in the backseat, hearing my grandmother, like my grandfather a proud immigrant from Italy, yelling at her husband, "Speak American, dammit!" when he lapsed into Italian.

Schultz, mirroring most of his fellow-travelers on the Left, seems to believe that the "Green Economy" may be the answer to our overall energy needs, obviously not wanting to admit that petroleum is, and will continue, to be the primary product to "fuel" our economy. I mentioned above the solutions to achieving energy independence – they mostly center around oil, coal and natural gas, with such forms as solar, wind and battery technology providing only secondary alternatives. Synthetics such as gasohol and ethanol have proven cost-ineffective thus far, but they fatten the wallets of many corn farmers while also serving as a form of corporate welfare for some huge conglomerates.

Much like my former congressional colleague and GOP presidential candidate Ron Paul and Barack Obama, Ed Schultz thinks the best way to conduct foreign policy is strictly through diplomatic means. I say diplomacy only works when dealing with nations or entities that do not want to kill or enslave us; therefore, the Reagan Doctrine of "Peace through Strength" is the best preventative. The federal government *does* have a constitutional duty to provide national defense and protect our borders. Schultz's contrary take on this is that "global cooperation is the best weapon against rogue states and terrorists." Not hardly. I was only halfway kidding some time ago when, in response to a question of how to deal with the cancer of Islamofascism, I replied that maybe we should bomb Muslim holy sites such as Mecca and Medina. But, in actuality, I have never ordered anybody to be bombed like Barack Obama did in Libya or like the carnage caused by terrorists on those passenger jets on 9-11.

I could go on and on about Ed Schultz and the other fact-challengers at MSNBC, but I do not need to – you get the message. Whether willing to admit it or not, these folks play fast and loose with facts, yet constantly accuse conservatives of doing it. Like most of the Lamestream Media – broadcast or print – they have been shameless cheerleaders for the Obama administration and other left-leaning politicians, but the worst thing is they pretend otherwise.

6

BARACK OBAMA, BILL AYERS AND OTHER 'DOMESTIC TERRORISTS'

When the trickle of disturbing information on the Fast and Furious gun-running scandal began to turn into a gushing faucet in 2011, it prompted me to write a column for *World Net Daily* in September of that year strongly suggesting that Congress consider articles of impeachment against President Barack Obama. That was not long after a friend had asked me if Obama was doing as badly as I had predicted he would, and I soberly replied, "No, much worse."

Unfortunately, for the country and its future, Obama again fooled enough people to get re-elected in November 2012, leaving all of us at the mercy of this dangerous radical for four more years. Now that he need not worry about trying to attract voters anymore, the 44th president has embarked on an even more-reckless journey than his disastrous first term, all the while dragging Americans with him as he shapes an almost-irrevocable legacy.

This is a subject not to be taken lightly and one to which I had given much thought as repeated illegalities or constitutional indiscretions unfolded in just the first three years of the Obama presidency – the gun-running fiasco being only one of many. Even though I fully realized that Obama would face voters once more, because the number of the president's actions that arguably qualified as impeachable offenses was staggering, the burning question before the country was what to do about it before the next election. What I felt then demands even more urgency today. Will we collectively be able to survive another three-plus years without the exceptional country that took more than two centuries to create being totally destroyed – morally, fiscally and otherwise?

Since he first took office in 2009, Obama has demonstrated repeated contempt for the Constitution and is increasingly resorting to rule by decree, having issued well over 100 executive orders, and counting. He has surrounded himself with more than 40 policy "czars," to whom even several Cabinet secretaries have become subordinate. These czars, many of them "recess appointments," put into place when Congress is out of session – or even in session, rendering appointments illegal -- are therefore totally unaccountable, having bypassed the constitutional process of advise-and-consent by not being confirmed by the U.S. Senate.

When I wrote the aforementioned column, I said it was time for the House of Representatives to take its constitutional responsibility seriously and launch an impeachment investigation. The investigative committee should hold hearings, collect and weigh the evidence, and then present its findings to the Congress and the nation. I still contend there is much evidence that says Obama has committed "high crimes and misdemeanors" that warrant impeachment and removal.

Among critical questions to justify impeachment on constitutional grounds are the following (but not limited only to these):

-- Did President Obama have personal knowledge of "Fast and Furious"?

-- Did the president have knowledge of the ongoing effort by Attorney General Eric Holder and other Justice Department officials to cover up the purpose and scope of this ill-conceived illegal project, which resulted in the killing of U.S. Border Patrol agent Brian Terry?

-- Did the president direct his appointees on the National Labor Relations Board to bring a lawsuit against Boeing Corp. as a political payoff to organized labor?

-- Did the president act contrary to the advice of his own CIA director, four previous intelligence agency heads of both parties and numerous experts on covert operations when, on April 16, 2009, he made public four internal Justice Department memos on terrorist interrogation techniques, thereby deliberately emasculating our anti-terrorist intelligence operations and endangering the lives of many intelligence agents?

-- Did the president have knowledge of a plan by the Department of Homeland Security, ordered by that agency's chief, Janet Napolitano, and the deputy commissioner of U.S. Customs and Border Protection, David Aguilar, to distort and falsify CBP's southwest border illegal-alien apprehension numbers by means of a deliberate, planned undercount – for the purpose of misleading the public and Congress about the true (abysmal) state of border security?

-- By choosing not to secure the border against unlawful entry, has the president willfully disregarded his clear duty under Article IV, Section 4, of the Constitution to protect the states from foreign invasion? Did the president admit this in a candid exchange with then-Sen. Jon Kyl, telling him the reason he was not stopping the cross-border human trafficking was to force congressional Republicans to strike a deal for amnesty legislation?

-- Is the president showing contempt for the Constitution, the separation of powers and the rule of law by ordering an "administrative amnesty" for millions of illegal aliens through the implementation of the John Morton memo of June 2011? (Morton was director of Immigration and Customs Enforcement, or ICE.)

-- Has the president demonstrated contempt for the Constitution and violated the separation of powers and the rule of law by issuing numerous executive orders and agency rules that have no basis in statute and often contradict congressional votes against such actions?

-- Did the president authorize then-Labor Secretary Hilda Solis to violate current federal laws against aiding and abetting illegal aliens by signing agreements with foreign countries and pledging to protect and fund educational efforts to inform illegal aliens of their workplace "rights"? Also, did these "agreements" she signed with foreign countries violate Article II, Section 2, of the Constitution, which clearly establishes the manner in which treaties are to be undertaken and ratified?

-- Did the president violate his oath of office when he instructed the Department of Justice not to defend the Defense of Marriage Act in federal courts? Does the Constitution permit the person designated by Article II, Section 1, as holding the "executive power" of government to decide unilaterally to not enforce a law with which he disagrees?

-- Did the president authorize or approve the offer of a federal job to Rep. Joe Sestak if he would withdraw from the 2010 Democrat primary race for U.S. Senate in Pennsylvania? And did the president proffer a similar offer to former state House Speaker Andrew Romanoff if he would not oppose appointed Sen. Michael Bennet in the 2010 Democrat primary in my home state of Colorado?

-- Did the president violate the War Powers Act by conducting military operations in Libya beyond the 60-day limitation and was he directly involved in deciding to reduce security forces, to issue a stand-down order and orchestrate an eventual cover-up and altered talking points on Benghazi?

-- Did the president know earlier than he publicly indicated in May 2013 about the Internal Revenue Service's and Department of Justice's apparently illegal activities respectively targeting Tea Party organizations and The Associated Press in ever-mushrooming scandals besetting his administration?

If President Obama is not guilty of any of these crimes, then a thorough investigation by a House committee with subpoena power will clear the air. If he is guilty, then the U.S. House of Representatives has a moral obligation to vote for a resolution of impeachment, and the U.S. Senate must bring him to trial.

Using the history of the nation's two presidential impeachment cases – Andrew Johnson and Bill Clinton – as a guide, there is no question that the impeachment and removal of Barack Obama is within the proper scope and purpose of the Constitution's impeachment provisions.

In March 2012, my friend and former fellow GOP colleague, North Carolina's Walter Jones, introduced an official resolution declaring that should the president use offensive military force without authorization of an act of Congress, "it is the sense of Congress" that such an act would be "an impeachable high crime and misdemeanor." Specifically, Article I, Section 8, of the Constitution reserves for Congress alone the power to declare war, a restriction that has been sorely tested in recent years, including Obama's authorization of military force in Libya. I contended that Jones introduced his resolution in response to startling comments from then-Defense Secretary Leon Panetta, who declared before the Senate Armed Services Committee that he and President Obama look not to the Congress for authorization to bomb Syria but to NATO and the United Nations. This led Jones to introduce his resolution; it eventually died because not enough so-called Republicans had the stomach to proceed according to constitutional guidelines. Maybe some will be so fed up that they will be more amenable to the idea again.

Questions posed herein all relate to actions affecting security and unlawful political intervention in executing our nation's laws – not mere policy differences -- and of course unnecessary American deaths in Libya. So on top of all the legitimate reasons I clearly cited for impeachment – not only of the president but of Attorney General Holder – are Obama's disastrous economic policies, his ideological war against domestic energy production and his other reckless proposals to add trillions to our national debt, the Obamacare mistake the worst of all. Such policies are not in themselves impeachable offenses, yet they all are damaging to our nation's well-being. But Obama's contempt for the Constitution and rule of law is a different matter altogether.

Why Barack Obama acts politically the way he does is easily explained; he provides the explanations in his own words – in not one, but two, purported autobiographies, which many in the know believe were ghost-written, even though the extremely narcissistic Obama is listed as the sole author of both books. *Dreams from My Father* was first published in 1995, when Obama was only 34, then re-published in 2004. *The Audacity of*

Hope was published in 2006, with the title taken from a sermon by Obama's two-decades-long black-liberation-theology pastor Jeremiah Wright, despite Obama basically throwing Wright under the bus for political expediency during the 2008 campaign.

It is widely believed by truly objective observers that Bill Ayers was the ghost-writer of *Dreams from My Father*, although no such credit is apparent anywhere in that regard, within the book itself or any outside references. Like the Rev. Wright, Ayers had been a longtime friend and fellow member of several boards with Obama on Chicago's South Side, and it was widely known that Ayers's living room was where the community organizer and future president announced his intention to run for the Illinois state Senate. However, also just as was the case with Wright, during the 2008 presidential campaign, Obama shrugged off the well-documented long association with the former self-avowed "domestic terrorist," Weather Underground and Students for a Democratic Society radical and public-building bomber, insisting quite disingenuously that Ayers merely was a casual acquaintance whom he had met only a few times. (It was revealed in March 2012 that a retired U.S. Postal Service letter-carrier who delivered mail to the Ayers family's suburban home for years had signed an affidavit attesting to conversations with Bill Ayers's mother telling him the family was financially assisting the college education of a "foreign student," and that the student was Barack Hussein Obama. That story, predictably, never has appeared in the mainstream media, which seemed to believe that 2012 was 2008 all over again regarding this radical politician and their blatant and shameless manner of providing cover for him. If it were not for independent investigative journalists like Dr. Jerome Corsi, who broke the "mailman" story, the public most likely would never hear of these serious shenanigans by Obama and those who protect him and his radical friends.)

Ayers himself otherwise earned his many of his writing chops during a two-year period. In 1999, he wrote a chapter, "To the Bone: Reflections in Black and White," as a response to the book's author in *Racism Explained to My Daughter* by Tahar Ben Jelloun. Ayers at the time was a faculty member at the University of Illinois at Chicago who, up to that point, had authored *Teaching for Social Justice, City Kids, City Teachers, A Kind and Just Parent* and *To Teach*. Two years after contributing to the Jelloun work, Ayers in 2001 completed with wife and fellow 1960s-'70s radical domestic terrorist Bernardine Dohrn and brother Rick Ayers *Zero Tolerance: Resisting the Drive for Punishment in Our Schools*, followed by his *tour de force* and personal *coup de grace*, his memoir titled *Fugitive Days*. In any case, all of Bill Ayers's writings are laced with a predictable mixture of anti-establishment screeds, anti-gun rhetoric, pro-homosexual encouragement and white-baiting, reverse-racist ramblings. One who reads the other Ayers products can readily realize a commonality in writing style and political/socio-economic philosophy when venturing through Obama's first book, lending credence to those who argue that Ayers was at least a co-author if not an outright ghost-writer. What is additionally curious about the Ayers brothers and their violent turns of radicalism is that, like movie director

Oliver Stone (who was discussed in a previous chapter), they grew up in a well-to-do white household in an upscale Chicago suburb, not in poverty or as a beleaguered minority.

Dreams from My Father offers revealing insights about Barack Hussein Obama's tortuous journey and how he reached what many consider the ultimate pinnacle as the world's most powerful man. Most shocking – but not surprising to me – are his anecdotes regarding formulation of decidedly Marxist ideas, coupled with the prism through which he views race issues as the son of a largely absentee Kenyan father and a Kansas-born white mother who fashioned herself as a free spirit. After his initial schooling in a Muslim-run academy in his Indonesian stepfather's native land, Obama finished his primary and secondary education in Hawaii, under the guardianship of his quite-progressive maternal grandparents. As he matured before first matriculating at California's Occidental College, Obama was taken under the wing of an older man – to whom he only refers in the book as "Frank" – named Frank Marshall Davis. The latter, it turns out, was an active member of the Communist Party, so the president's evolution into a Chicago community organizer, whose "bibles" were Saul Alinsky's *Rules for Radicals* and *The Communist Manifesto*, and eventually an ultra-left elected official, was predictable and self-fulfilling. New Zealand-based author/researcher Trevor Loudon revealed in his 2012 book, *Barack Obama and the Enemies Within,* that it was Davis who lured Obama to Chicago after having helped enable him in his higher-education pursuits as a Marxist acolyte. Loudon's research also evidenced that an extreme-left Illinois state senator named Alice Palmer paved a path for each step of the future president's political career. Yet, the mainstream media went to great lengths to cover up all of this in 2008.

Obama had decided during his teen-age years that he wanted nothing to do with the white half of his *id*; he would thereafter identify not only wholly as a black man, but moreover as a radical one. His self-admitted being was influenced by such writers and philosophers as Richard Wright, James Baldwin and black-nationalist leader Malcolm X. The newly created, or transformed, self-realization included incorporation of fear and distrust of whites, with a toxic mixture of Marxism thrown in for good measure. Obama asks rhetorically in his first book: "How could America send men into space and still keep its black citizens in bondage?" This is ridiculous and patently absurd in the 1960s and '70s when he was growing up, especially in light of the *Brown v. Board of Education* U.S. Supreme Court desegregation decision in 1954 and the 1964 Civil Rights Act. It is the typical thinking of a radical leftist historical revisionist like this president.

Barack Obama further writes of his maternal grandfather as having a "desire ... to obliterate the past (and) this confidence in the possibility of remaking the world from whole cloth (which) proved to be his most lasting patrimony." Indeed, because all this aptly describes present-day Obama and *his* desire to do the same with his own obfuscated past regarding the string of hidden and yet-to-be-released documentation from all aspects of his life that we expect a president of the United States to freely provide for the complete historical record.

As for the modern history of Japanese-Americans being interned without due process during World War II, as Obama cites in *Dreams*, I would remind him that this was perpetrated by another Democrat president like himself.

Struggling early with his mixed racial reality as he approached young adulthood in Honolulu, Obama admits, "Away from my mother, away from my grandparents, I was engaged in a fitful interior struggle. I was trying to raise myself to be a black man in America, and beyond the given of my appearance, no one around me seemed to know exactly what that means." But apparently, based on Obama's own writings, he was most profoundly influenced by Frank the Communist and self-avowed Black Power advocate, as greatly evidenced by how the former turned out.

Using Davis's guidance as a model, Obama evolved into a left-wing campus activist at Occidental, honing his not-so-underlying Marxist machinations before sharpening them to an even harsher edge by the time he arrived at New York's Columbia University. He purportedly completed his undergraduate education at Columbia, eventually entering Harvard Law School, although all this is based on faith since, as mentioned, presence of transcripts and other records is sparse. Therefore, it is easy to revise history by the seat of your pants, whether it be the personal variety or that affecting everyone else in the world by default. I have visited several presidential libraries around the country and have truly wondered, based on the well-documented cradle-to-grave stories of some of the 20th century's foremost leaders, what Barack Obama's "library" will look like, devoid of such necessary input.

As for *The Audacity of Hope*, by the time it was published, two years after he was elected to the U.S. Senate, Barack Obama already had lost a Democrat congressional primary to ex-Black Panther and incumbent Bobby Rush, my former House colleague, and then was an elected Illinois state senator, having been groomed for the latter job by predecessor/mentor Alice Palmer. So Obama was no longer officially a community organizer on the streets of Chicago, but had taken the same tactics into the state Capitol – that is other than on the many occasions when he voted "Present" to avoid leaving a trail of possibly controversial Yea or Nay votes that could haunt him later in his political career. As a revisionist, when much of your life lacks sufficient documentation to create a genuine public record, is not difficult to always vote Present.

Audacity is an appropriate word to be in the title because Obama was truly audacious enough to detail in his second book's pages ideas or plans which he had no intention to carry out, once elected president. Much to the contrary, and in typical Obama fashion, in *Audacity*, he quite often makes statements that are the exact opposite of his true aims. As an adjunct to *Dreams*, in terms of continuing with the autobiographical bent, I find it extremely curious and questionable that Obama, in 2006, set the tone for essentially whitewashing his established long relationships with Bill Ayers and Jeremiah Wright – the same way his deep links to the likes of Davis and Palmer were downplayed.

Here is something funny, in a strictly ironic sense, and indicative of what I mean: Barack Obama has always said how, save sports events, he never watches television, especially shows that feature political talking heads. Yet in *Audacity*, he writes: "When I see Ann Coulter or Sean Hannity baying across the television screen, I find it hard to take them seriously; I assume that they must be saying what they do primarily to boost book sales or ratings, although I wonder who would spend their precious evenings with such sourpusses." That explains, then, why the president has repeatedly rebuffed Hannity's invitations to appear on his nightly program or at least share a brew with the Fox News host like he found time to do when he "refereed" the Beer Summit with the vice president, Obama friend Henry Louis Gates and the Cambridge, Mass., police officer who had arrested Gates in a widely misreported and misportrayed incident early in his first term.

In his infinite knowledge of all things (in his own mind, of course) – despite no real practical knowledge or experience at all -- Barack Obama did it again in March 2012 when he felt compelled to insinuate himself into the tragic, non-federal death of Florida teen-ager Trayvon Martin on Feb. 26. In a strictly local incident that evolved quickly into a racially tinged internationally sensationalized affair, Martin was fatally shot by neighborhood-watchman George Zimmerman near a gated community in the Orlando suburb of Sanford. When Sanford police did not arrest or file charges against Zimmerman, citing application of Florida's "Stand Your Ground" law regarding self-defense on private property, the case went viral on the Internet, and every race-hustler came out of the wall screaming "racism," as is *de rigueur* for radical reverse-racists, who then find the sizable misinformed segment of the public already gathering nationwide in lockstep compliance. As the case continued to develop, fact after fact came to light; among them:

> --The shooter, George Zimmerman, according to evidence leaked from authorities, and corroborated by at least one eyewitness, did not instigate action following a 911 call he had placed about a suspicious character in a "hoodie," and had followed police instructions not to confront the suspect. Then, as evidence uncovered by a local reporter further showed, Martin pursued Zimmerman as the watchman tried to climb back into his vehicle. Finally, a scuffle ensued and amid the wrestling match, Zimmerman fatally shot Martin, who incidentally had been cradling items, that appeared to potentially be a

weapon but were a beverage container and candy bag.

-- The mainstream media, in typical fashion, and long before any facts were in, became instant judge and jury, castigating the Sanford authorities, casting Martin as an unfortunate, defenseless victim and universally portraying Zimmerman as some sort of -racist, Old West vigilante on the prowl for young black skins. NBC News was forced to apologize and fired the culpable employee for doctoring the audio tape of the watchman's 911 call to report suspicious activity; the tape was doctored to make Zimmerman sound like a racist bent on killing innocent blacks. Turns out George Zimmerman, by accounts of friends and acquaintances who were interviewed and publicly defended him (some of them black), is a giving member of the community who, rather than a lily-white vigilante, is a generally law-abiding citizen of half-Peruvian descent who also has black family members.

-- Conversely, the photos of Trayvon Martin as a smiling, docile child that radical race-baiters in the mainstream media were publicizing with their typically slanted stories now seem to be fiction. Then, on my website, tomtancredo.com, I posted photos, provided by credible sources, of a more-recent Trayvon Martin, the 6-foot-plus one with a record of school suspensions, drug use and gang activity – hardly the innocent young lad presented by everyone from his parents to biased reporters to Al Sharpton and Jesse Jackson.

All of this naturally did not deter the president of the United States, our radical-in-chief, from weighing in. Obama declared about Martin, "If I had a son, he would have looked like Trayvon." Then he proceeded, a la the Cambridge affair, to give his opinion on a *local* criminal case that would not be fully adjudicated until midsummer 2013, and the vile double standard was at work again, with the occupant of the White House joining the choir of voices calling for Zimmerman's hide. I mean, even though Obama was a mere U.S. senator and presidential candidate in March 2008, why did he – and Sharpton, and Jackson – then not utter a word of horror regarding the random gang shooting of an apparently innocent, Stanford-bound athlete, Jamiel Shaw, Jr., on a South Los Angeles street? Is it because young Shaw was not the kind of black held in "esteem" by the radical, politically correct crowd, being that he was law-abiding, a good student and a respected athlete? The taste of these folks runs more toward convicted cop-killers, whom they prop up as martyrs in a manner associated with the double standard wherein genuine good becomes soulless evil, and vice-versa.

Also revealing were "tweets" from Martin's Twitter account – they indicated a definite lean toward usage of assorted "gangsta" *patois*, including liberal dollops of variations of the "N" word and certain anatomical references. This is not the type of language normally employed by someone regarded as "a nice young man," regardless of color or ethnic standing.

In an op-ed column on March 27, 2012, I wrote: "Liberals are hypocrites. This is the Trayvon Martin that the media wants you to see ... young, innocent, full of life and hope. But that's that's not the whole picture, nor is it a CURRENT picture." I went on to say that the aforementioned photos spoke for themselves. I mentioned that the same, race-selective media, save the Chicago Tribune, and the Sharpton-Jackson coterie, totally ignored a more-recent story of 10 people (including a 6-YEAR-OLD GIRL) gunned down in Chicago by a group of black gang members. I asked if this was hypocrisy – which it was – but let readers decide for themselves.

The day before my column, another pundit, Washington, D.C.-based Peter Bradley, suggested in his own op-ed that George Zimmerman was a modern victim of a "lynching," one incited by the Obama White House, despite no charges filed against the watchman. Bradley also criticized the "Righteous Right," which, he said, "rolled over on its back like a spaniel." Bradley further detailed, beyond the Chicago killing spree, several varied slayings and serious crimes that warranted attention but which the Lamestream Media and shakedown artists ignored because they were not politically correct. Bottom line for Bradley: "Black-on-black crime can be officially, albeit discreetly, deplored. ... But blacks must never be cast as the perpetrators of hate crimes – even though they are easily the most prominent perpetrators of racial violence."

Zimmerman was acquitted of all charges by a six-woman jury in July 2013 amid the lurking threats of massive race riots and possible further later prosecution.

In his second book, Obama sets the stage for future revamping of the health-care and education systems by talking around his precise plan, yet dropping subtle hints along the way about ensuring equal outcomes and "investing," or code for racial quotas and excessive, runaway spending. We can readily see what has transpired since, as any legitimate criticism of the Obama administration has resulted in charges of racism and an already-bloated national debt has ballooned to a record $16 trillion-plus under the same regime.

Again demonstrating what we would all come to know as his inherent hypocrisy, Obama states, "Ultimately … I believe any attempt by Democrats to pursue a more sharply partisan and ideological strategy misapprehends the moment we're in. I am convinced that whenever we exaggerate or demonize, oversimplify or overstate our case, we lose. Whenever we dumb down the political debate, we lose." Yes, Mr. President, that certainly explains your environmental extremism, your appointments of two judicial zealots to the Supreme Court and, worst of all, the so-called health-care "reform" that you shoved down our collective throats – all during your first term.

It is too bad that Barack Obama professes to believe in moral values, as he writes in *Audacity*, but avoids them whenever possible. "I think Democrats are wrong to run away from a debate about values, as wrong as those conservatives who see values only as a wedge to pry loose working-class voters from the Democratic base," he states. Yet bear in mind when a liberal Democrat mentions "working-class" people, he means those who belong to a union, relegating non-union wage-earners to status as not-so-hard-working but ripe for involuntarily paying taxes and dues that ultimately fund unions and other less-worthy programs. It represents confiscatory redistribution at its worst.

Barack Obama's non-résumé résumé lists the one steady occupation he held as a non-collegiate adult – other than that of a community organizer or elected state and U.S. senator – as a constitutional law professor. However, evidence otherwise indicates he was merely a part-time lecturer on constitutional law. To assess how someone with such latent, or maybe not-so-hidden, Marxist tendencies has approached the Constitution – from his writings in theory in *Audacity* to his practical application, especially as president – you have to conclude his understanding of this seminal document is quite warped.

Throughout the second book are two disturbing consistencies: Constant reference to our venerable constitutional republic as a "democracy," and the "living" nature of our Constitution, as if it were a flexible, malleable document. While we vote at virtually every level in democratic, one-person, one-vote fashion, the beauty of the federalist system the Founders created lies in republican principles that allow both states and individuals to exercise enumerated rights free of interference by a central government. If we were a democracy, as Obama and other lefty radicals believe, we would have to put up with a Congress that more resembles the run-amok, multi-party legislative bodies of all the world's parliamentary countries. Instead of their constant zeal for changing the U.S. Constitution by fiat via their self-chosen judicial activists in black robes – most notably in decisions in response to, and contrary to, recent free elections – members of the Left must begin to soberly realize that the process for amending the Constitution is challenging for obvious reasons.

What Barack Obama and his minions are consciously doing on a daily basis is "shredding" our most-cherished document, bit-by-bit. Like the Bible, they regard the Constitution as just another collection of historical accounts. Similar to their disdain for American Exceptionalism, they insist that, rather than follow the Constitution as the ultimate and appropriate guide for the rule of law, our citizens instead must be subjected to the whims of "international law" as the preeminent standard. According to Obama, as written in *The Audacity of Hope*, his "answer" requires "a shift in metaphors, one that sees our democracy not as a house to be built, but as a conversation to be had." His interpretation of the conversation is one-way in nature – having liberal judges change common-sense laws, as formulated by the Framers, or election results, to suit their own revisionist needs, much to the detriment of American society as a whole.

Of course, Obama is not the first Democrat president to view the U.S. Constitution as a routine piece of paper ripe for revision. The seeds for using the prime document as a plaything by presidents of that party were

160

planted by Woodrow Wilson in the early 20th century, then sown in the 1930s by Franklin Roosevelt. In his excellent book, *Ameritopia*, published in 2012, Mark Levin discusses a wishful, 1908 treatise, by Wilson, *Constitutional Government in the United States*, written five years before he entered the Oval Office. Writes Levin: "… Wilson wrote not of the Constitution as is but as he wished it to be – that is, denuded of its carefully crafted limits on the central government."

Watching a riveting, 1 ½-hour documentary, *Agenda: Grinding America Down*, written, produced and directed by former Idaho state legislator Curtis Bowers, one gets deep insight into the denizens who are entrenched into every nook and cranny of the Obama regime, and exactly the dangerous designs in their diabolical minds.

Here are some of the accurate conclusions about Obama and Co. as portrayed by Bowers in his 2011 film, provided by varied credible observers, including the author himself:

> -- As a graduate student at another college, Bowers attended a conference at the University of California at Berkeley in summer 1992 for fact-finding purposes. The facts, as he soon discovered, were that the Berkeley attendees naturally fostered a decidedly socialist agenda, termed "microwave socialism" by Bowers – in other words, put redistributive baked goods into a hot mini-oven, then watch them be zapped into edible Marxism. "They promoted

cohabitation instead of traditional marriage, plus getting behind the environmental movement to destroy business, and to destroy culture and morality, (encouraging) Americans to accept homosexuality. ... In retrospect, they were successful in subverting traditional American values and achieving stated goals," he said. The bottom-line implication, Bowers correctly determined, is "if we lose our Judeo-Christian framework, we're lost forever."

-- A 1958 book, *The Naked Communist*, by late former FBI agent W. Cleon Skousen, detailed what eventually would happen -- and has horrifyingly begun to occur in the daily excesses of the Obama administration, with outside, left-wing special interests setting policy by calling the shots, or others in middle- to high-level administration posts, including lifetime federal judgeships. Among goals mentioned by Skousen that already have been realized are elimination of prayer in schools, the strong push to have obscenity legitimized, control of the mass media and infiltration of places of worship. It is truly scary to envision what the next four years will bring, now that the electorate has accorded Obama and Co. virtual *carte blanche* for unbridled revisions of our day-to-day existence.

--In his documentary, Bowers asked influential people: "Is communism dead?" Sadly, a largely consensus answer was, "No," for the above-stated and other reasons.

-- Another author cited by Bowers was John Stormer, who wrote *None Dare Call It Treason* in 1964, followed in 1990 by *None Dare Call It Treason ...25 Years Later*. In analogous fashion, Stormer, a pastor, former school superintendent and ardent anti-communist, wrote: "A good magician raises his hand to his ear, while doing all his dirty work with the other hand." Method lesson, then, with our current coterie of Marxist "magicians," always keep an eagle eye on their *other* hand.

-- Bowers also asked rhetorically, "What's so bad about communism?", then replied himself, "Mass murder of more people than all other economic and political systems combined, enslavement, oppression – the exact opposite of stated goals." Strangely similar to the *modus operandi* of Barack Hussein Obama and his fellow-travelers.

-- One of the most-brutal practitioners of *The Communist Manifesto*, Vladimir Ilyich Lenin, was blunt and frank when he said, "Communism is a form of socialism. The goal of socialism is communism." Although not mentioned in *Agenda*, another famous, and telling, quote from Lenin is "A lie told often enough becomes the truth." Are you listening, Mr. Obama, fellow Democrats and compliant members of the Lamestream Media who are nothing more than Lenin's Useful Idiots? Sounds a lot like all of you, does it not? The 2008 and 2012 elections proved that mud will stick to the wall if enough is slung.

-- Before Lenin's ascension, the Fabian Socialists, in 1883 in England, upon the death of Karl Marx, grabbed the red baton and set out a path for all their successors. Less than a century later, in 1960s America, this led ultimately to Students for a Democratic Society and other like-minded radicals. As these creatures aged, they branched out -- one-time SDS member Jim Wallis, a self-professed man of the cloth whose real religion is Marxism, and the aforementioned Bill Ayers, to cite two prime examples.

-- The big, always-underlying idea was "to make America so corrupt, it stinks," which is readily apparent with today's "feminazis": Destroy the family, starting by tearing down patriarchal society and supplanting it with government as a nanny. Breaking down of cultural traditions make it easy. As I have said often, morality simply is having the character to do what you *should* do, not what you are forced to do. The constant march toward permanent socialism and Marxism is all part of an incremental revolution from within, as laid out in the thousands of pages written by Italian communist kingpin Antonio Gramsci in the 1930s, and "refined" four decades later in Saul Alinsky's *Rules for Radicals*. As mentioned in *Agenda*, the ties between the two were so profound, despite the wide time gap, that Alinsky dedicated his book to Gramsci, describing him as the first anti-establishment activist.

-- In between Gramsci, Alinsky and the 2008 election of Obama were the advent and evolution of the Cloward-Piven "crisis strategy" employed by leftists, especially community organizers like Alinsky and the current president. This was played out in spades when current Chicago Mayor Rahm Emanuel, Obama's first White House chief of staff, declared, "Never let a crisis go to waste." (The crisis strategy was devised by a social-activist, heterosexual married couple [a liberal novelty], Richard Cloward and Frances Fox-Piven, in the 1960s.) Also, any time left-wingers want to challenge the Constitution or some election result with which they disagree, they first "shop around" for a sympathetic court venue, then they sic mad-dog activist lawyers from some

foaming-at-the-mouth entity such as the
American Civil Liberties Union or Southern
Poverty Law Center on the case.

(Further anecdotes from *Agenda*, specifically
regarding the Left's deleterious effect on education, will
be discussed in the next chapter.)

In addition to the already detailed list of possible
impeachable offenses over the past four years, major
indiscretions, constitutional violations and assorted
insults visited upon an either uninformed or unwilling
citizenry have been committed by the reigning
administration. To wit:

> -- Outside of Obamacare and its multi-
> trillion-dollar embarrassment of trying to
> dismantle a flawed – but still the world's best
> -- health-care apparatus, the biggest-buck
> single boondoggle has been the Solyndra
> scandal. More than a half-billion dollars of
> taxpayer money was used to fund a faulty
> solar-energy firm that not much later declared
> bankruptcy. In addition, of course, prior to
> that were the failed Stimulus and Cash for
> Clunkers programs, along with Dodd-Frank
> so-called financial reforms that were passed
> when both houses of Congress had Democrat
> majorities before the 2010 elections.
>
> -- In December 2011, The Heritage
> Foundation issued its 32-Month Report Card

of the Obama administration, and the findings in roughly four dozen areas were, to say the least, shocking. Among highlights, this president was the first in history: to preside over a cut in the nation's credit rating; to require all Americans to purchase a product from a third party; to demand a company hand over $20 billion to one of his political appointees; to have signed a law by auto-pen without being present; to arbitrarily declare an existing law unconstitutional and refuse to enforce it; to tell a major manufacturing company in which state it is allowed to locate a factory; to publicly bow to America's enemies while refusing to salute the U.S. flag; to abrogate bankruptcy law to turn over control of companies to his union supporters; and to terminate America's ability to put a man in space. That is just a partial list, but I think you get the drift.

Some of the most-egregious missteps (to use a kind word) under Barack Obama have been on the environmental front, the Solyndra mess notwithstanding, under the firm, dictatorial grip of extremists Carol Browner, Obama's first Environmental Czar, and her lackey, Lisa Jackson, former head of the Environmental Protection Agency (EPA). (Browner was recycled to re-terrorize America with her screwy and dangerous "green" notions after her initial reign of terror as Bill Clinton's EPA director in the 1990s.) Here again is an abbreviated list of some of the worst examples foisted upon the country by the Browner-Jackson cabal:

> -- After the April 2011 Gulf of Mexico BP oil spill, the president, on the ill-timed advice of then-Interior Secretary Ken Salazar, another green zealot from my home state of Colorado, issued an executive order that shut drilling in the gulf for months. The result choked the economies of the five Gulf Coast states and stymied interstate and international commerce.

> -- The administration endorsed the United Nations Agenda 21 in 2011, paving the way for "smart growth" policies and international sovereignty over domestic energy, environmental decisions and the Law of the Sea, thus effectively stripping our own sovereign nation of its ability to stand alone even on the most-obvious issues where we were correct and, well, exceptional.

> -- President Obama, in November 2011, announced a delay in the important Keystone XL pipeline, which, when completed, would transport oil from western Canada's rich tar sands to Texas refineries. His stated reason for the delay was potential damage to Nebraska's Sand Hills. However, Cornhusker State officials wisely did not wait long to oppose Obama's move, quickly offering a route change that would bypass the Sand

Hills. Then, after the Nebraska route revision two months later, Obama reiterated that there would be no pipeline, at least until 2013, or conveniently beyond the 2012 presidential balloting. Despite that election being about jobs and the economy, this miscast so-called leader of the free world would nevertheless ignore those facts and cater instead to Marxist-dominated purported environmental interests simply to consolidate power even further. A study quoted by *Powerline Blog* during the same month Obama issued his initial announcement concluded that Keystone would create somewhere between a quarter- and a half-million permanent new jobs while moderating oil prices – all to the obliviousness of the "Jobs President." (When Democrats say something about "jobs," they do not mean creation of them – unless they are part-time and without benefits – but net loss of meaningful full-time positions by over-regulating and over-taxing many employers out of business.)

-- In an Oct. 21, 2011, op-ed column in the *Los Angeles Times*, Lisa Jackson accused House Republicans of undermining the EPA she headed by trying to dismantle environmental laws. She termed GOP efforts as "too dirty to fail" and strongly implied that the opposing party advocated elimination of clean air and clean water – simultaneous, but not non-coincidental, to a disgusting

Democratic National Committee national TV ad that showed Republicans shoving a wheelchair-bound grandmother off a cliff to deny her health care. Jackson's column, while claiming not to be hyperbolic, attempted to draw an "irrefutable" link "between health issues and pollution," never conceding that health problems generally are more complex than that. The key, of course, is to remember that, aside from sheer power grabs and redistributive money-shuffling with taxpayers always unwittingly footing the bill, any "jobs" program has nothing to do with the environment and public health but everything to do with creating and perpetuating union and government jobs, and beefing up the Left's increasingly deathly grip on power and individual liberties.

-- Jackson's EPA, in conjunction with the National Highway Traffic Safety Administration, also proposed in fall 2011, an unrealistic goal of a fleet-wide fuel economy average of 54.5 miles per gallon by 2025, thus bloating the average new-car price by thousands of dollars, according to a Heritage Foundation study. The Heritage findings also accurately showed that because average vehicle size would be greatly reduced to achieve unrealistic fuel standards, "another unacceptable consequence is loss of life resulting from smaller vehicles."

-- In a pathetic display of "in your face" to
the American people, Obama, on Jan. 11,
2012, strode to the podium, with
teleprompters in tow, to thank the EPA (For
what? Meddling needlessly in our daily
lives?) and call the agency "vital." Standing
by his side gloating was Lisa Jackson.

The number of unaccountable "czars" appointed in
this administration's first three years is staggering – 45 at
last count. They have ranged from AIDS Czar Jeffrey
Crowley to Auto Recovery Czar Ed Montgomery to
California Water Czar David J. Hayes, and also included
recently deposed and ineffective Border Czar Alan Bersin.
Shown the door in 2010 was controversial Green Jobs
Czar Van Jones, a self-avowed communist whose big push
was dubbed "The Green Collar Economy," which was
described in 2008 in an eponymous book on the subject.
(It was announced in summer 2013 that Jones would be
one of two liberals facing two conservatives in the
reintroduction of CNN's *Crossfire*.)

"Why would the Russians want to be putting spies
in (the Obama) White House?" radio talk star Rush
Limbaugh once asked his listeners upon Jones's
departure. "Most of his czars are already communists."

Other than those mentioned above, perhaps the
most-dangerous is Cass Sunstein, President Obama's
former Regulatory Czar, who possessed likely the greatest
clout among any Obama adviser, save the president's wife
or his creepy counselor who keeps her man schooled in the

Chicago Way, Valerie Jarrett. When Obama climbs aboard Air Force One on another campaign trip or one of his all-too-frequent taxpayer-funded vacations, that bespectacled woman with the short *coif* always accompanying him is the ever-ubiquitous Jarrett; Michelle, and Bo the presidential dog, usually leave for the same junkets on separate jets also subsidized by the Average Joe and squandering enormous amounts of jet fuel (which would make Lisa Jackson and Carol Browner cringe if a Republican First Lady were perpetrating such waste.) Jarrett, incidentally, was a longtime close associate and philosophical soul mate of Alice Palmer, according to New Zealand-based researcher/blogger Trevor Loudon.

Let there be no doubt from whence Sunstein and his Marxist philosophy have emanated; he has written more than a dozen books on virtually every public-policy topic under the Sun. The titles themselves are usually quite prophetic and self-fulfilling. Books authored by Sunstein between 1990 and 2009 include *After the Rights Revolution*; *The Partial Constitution*; *Democracy and the Problem of Free Speech*; *Legal Reasoning and Political Conflict*; *Free Markets and Social Justice*; *One Case at a Time*; *Republic.com*; *Designing Democracy*; *Risk and Reason*; and *Why Societies Need Dissent*. Plus, he co-authored a small handful of other works.

However, Sunstein's two most revolutionary and controversial volumes have been 2004's *The Second Bill of Rights: FDR's Unfinished Revolution and Why We Need It More Than Ever* and the 2005 *Radicals in Robes: Why Extreme Right-Wing Courts Are Wrong for America*. As evidenced by the first title, Sunstein, despite being officially out of the loop, still is in a position to cajole Obama into replicating Franklin D. Roosevelt's massive dose of socialism that dominated America from 1932 until World War II broke out. The aim of the second book already has been achieved in real time with the placement of Sonia Sotomayor and Elena Kagan on the U.S. Supreme Court and scores of like-minded leftists at the lower federal jurisdictions – all lifetime appointments that will forever affect every American's existence. Now that Obama has earned a second term, conservatives (and any other decent, reasonable citizens) need to pray that none of the current "originalist" Supreme Court justices die or retire on the current presidential watch. Sunstein, with characteristic delusion, lamented that the liberal element "had all but disappeared" on the nation's highest court, despite the presence at the time of John Paul Stevens, David Souter, Stephen Breyer and Ruth Bader Ginsburg. Lest there be any doubt of an ultra-liberal infusion of judicial activists who have disdain for the Constitution, simply look at Sotomayor and Kagan, coupled with the ongoing living specter of Breyer and Bader Ginsburg.

On Jan. 10, 2012, joining Sunstein as one of the president's right hands – in a shamefully patronizing attempt to curry favor with Hispanics – was newly appointed domestic policy adviser Cecilia Muñoz. Muñoz had been a longtime left-wing, race-conscious radical at the highest levels of an illegal alien-coddling group, *the National Council of La Raza*. Major goals of this group include amnesty, legalization and voting rights for illegals, plus totally open borders. Naturally, other than Obama himself, the leading voice in the White House for the U.S.

Senate Gang of Eight amnesty-without-security proposal is open-borders advocate Cecilia Muñoz.

Even though Sunstein himself had officially departed, by spring 2013, the president nominated Sunstein's wife, Samantha Power, a self-avowed Palestinian sympathizer and Israel arch-critic, to be U.S. ambassador to the United Nations. Unfortunately, a spineless majority in the U.S. Senate confirmed Power in August 2013.

One who thinks as I do would hope that, come November 2016, after we all awake from the national nightmare of Sunstein's and Muñoz's patron at 1600 Pennsylvania Avenue, we will install at least some common-sense conservative who can contribute to smothering such hateful, shrill voices of radical revisionists now haunting and taunting us.

7

JAY BENNISH, WARD CHURCHILL

AND THE ACADEMIC BRAINWASHERS

There is an insidious, anti-patriotic monster that has slithered into our nation's classrooms and worked its way into the minds of our children. It comes in the innocent-appearing façade of such apparently non-threatening aspects as political correctness, diversity and social justice. It is underscored by the subliminal, and sometimes not-so-hidden, veritable brainwashing of pupils as young as pre-school age. It shows up in nearly every textbook, or supplemental text, approved these days by liberal-dominated public boards of education and "progressive" operators of private and supposedly parochial schools.

This propaganda and indoctrination that runs rampant in our educational system at every level is a more-recent phenomenon – perhaps the past two decades. Yet I can personally cite instances that go back beyond that threshold. For instance, I can clearly remember one situation when I was an official with the U.S. Department of Education (an agency, by the way, which, as I mentioned in Chapter 5, should never have been created and long ago should have been eliminated). It was sometime in the mid-1980s, during the Reagan administration. We were present at a mostly minority school, in Manhattan, not far from Harlem, for what was called a Blue Ribbon Schools ceremony. We all stood, and everyone was asked to sing in unison first the "Black National Anthem," followed immediately by the "Puerto Rican National Anthem." Not once was the "Star Spangled Banner" played. I asked myself, "Isn't this America?" and thought, "I didn't even know there was a Black National Anthem or a Puerto Rican National Anthem." Now, I ask myself as well, "Is it not our sacred duty to inculcate *all* American children, regardless of race, creed, color or social standing, with the spirit of patriotism and pride that accompany being, well, an American?" (BTW, not to brag, but I greatly reduced unnecessary staff in that federal post, realizing what a useless agency the Jimmy Carter-created Department of Education was.)

Fast-forward to a much more recent example of how anti-patriotic revisionists at least are trying to wreak havoc with our education apparatus.

On my weeknight radio talk show, broadcast out of Colorado Springs, Colo., not long ago, a young man named Mike Shaw, of Tucson, Ariz., recounted to me and my listeners the horrors of a racist, Latino group of activists using its muscle and bullying tactics to force its agenda on an unwilling majority. It is perhaps the most-egregious example I have seen in a long time in a public school. The movement to create a Mexican-American Studies program is fueled by *La Raza Unida*, which translates into English as The United Race. The idea behind this is to indoctrinate every student in the local district into the idea that much of the land in the U.S. Southwest was "stolen" by this country from Mexico. This despite the fact there was a conflict, the 1840s Mexican War, in which the United States, under all the acceptable battlefield conventions of the time, fairly and squarely won the right to that vast amount land, which Latino activists call *Aztlan*, a new independent country.

This is certainly a racist, and a clearly separatist, agenda. It is nothing but bizarre and whacko. These folks are intent on a movement to create this new country, carved out of several U.S. states. They would do so, if allowed, by forcing the rolling back of our borders to pre-Mexican War configurations, not unlike President Obama's 2011 push to have Israel cede all its territory to pre-1967 boundaries. Remember that present-day Israel includes lands won, also fair and square, in wars that resulted from the Israelis being attacked *first*. Real socialists, you see, operate in the same manner, regardless of venue, to justify their world-dominating machinations.

The racist aspect aside, all this is decidedly socialistic and communistic, with the trademark term of "social justice" imbuing itself into the overall picture. According to Shaw, a private businessman who is a county Republican Party official in Tucson, the move to create the

Mexican-American Studies curriculum district-wide is opposed even by sensible liberal Democrats who serve on the school board. "The (activists) want to implement the social justice curriculum into all class levels, whether the Mexican-American Studies is approved or not," he told my radio audience. He termed the whole ongoing controversy as "Bizarreland" and said he has videotaped and photographed evidence that deposed former University of Colorado ethnic-studies professor, and *faux*-Indian, Ward Churchill showed up in Tucson to egg on activists. This proves my point that this has everything to do with socialism and all its accouterments and nothing really to do with so-called "ethnic studies," since Churchill is a notorious socialist operative before anything else.

Notably, during a protest on the steps of the Arizona State Capitol in Phoenix, a group of African-American Studies students was let out of school to shout down Tom Horne, the Republican former state Superintendent of Public Instruction who in 2010 was elected Arizona's new attorney general. And speaking of the state laws which Horne is delegated with upholding, Senate Bill 1070, the Arizona statute that cracks down on illegal aliens, has become a lightning-rod issue for the critics, who now can unfortunately couple criticism of that law with new displeasure aimed at calling Arizona the ultimate racist state.

Personally, as someone who has been in the figurative foxholes for years leading the battle against anti-American forces who would dare threaten our borders and national security, I find any substitute curriculum centered around social justice as dangerous as the original-intent ethnic-studies curriculum it was designed to replace. In fact, I would dare venture the thought that the Mexican-American Studies ploy was nothing more than a ruse, or Trojan Horse, with the real aim from the outset being implementation of the social justice agenda. Remember always that "social justice" is nothing but a euphemism for communism and Marxism/Leninism.

Shaw, whom I spent two hours with at lunch on his May 2011 trip to Colorado to huddle with state lawmakers, is convinced of the same collusion, especially having witnessed and documented the Arizona appearance of rabble-rouser Churchill. Shaw believes their activities offer proof of like-minded thinking and that the same people work hand-in-hand, regardless of state, or even national, borders, to get their way.

According to the website of the state's largest newspaper, the *Arizona Republic*, *AZCentral.com*, the Tucson program already has been investigated for violating the law. The website detailed that an audit of the program found:

> -- Texts and other materials for junior-level courses referenced white people as "oppressors" and "oppressing" Hispanics.

> -- Curriculum and materials repeatedly emphasize the importance of building Hispanic nationalism and unity in the face of assimilation and oppression.

Despite these comments, the audit nonetheless also painted a rosy picture of the dubious proposed program. For instance, the audit by the Cambium Learning Group praised the program as promoting peace and racial harmony, and concluded that it did not exacerbate racial tension. All of which is astounding to Tom Horne's successor as state Superintendent of Public Instruction, fellow Republican John Huppenthal. Huppenthal totally rejected the audit's observations, further stating that he questioned whether it "was in fact an audit."

On its own website Cambium describes its mission thusly:

> "Cambium Learning Group, Inc. operates three business units: Voyager, a comprehensive intervention business; Sopris, a supplemental solutions business; and Cambium Learning Technologies, which includes ExploreLearning, IntelliTools, Kurzweil and Learning A-Z. Through its coredivisions, Cambium Learning Group, Inc. provides research-based education solutions for students in Pre-K through 12th grade, including intervention curricula, educational technologies and services primarily focused on serving the needs of the nation's most challenged learners and enabling students to reach their full potential."

(In December 2011, an administrative law judge ruled the proposed Tucson program invalid, although the decision was subject to appeal.)

Beyond the mundane, neutral tone of the Cambium mission statement, there is more than meets the eye, as the old saying goes.

Carolyn W. Getridge, Senior Vice President of Human Resources and Urban Development for Cambium, previously spent many years at the highest levels of education administration in the Oakland (Calif.) school district and in surrounding Alameda County. It is one of the nation's most-liberal areas and always has been an incubator for education "reform," where pupils as young as pre-school age are constantly used as figurative lab rats for one hare-brained experiment or another. Even though it would be problematical to blame someone like Ms. Getridge directly, the continuum of like-minded thinking prevails – as evidenced by the latest event in this regard, which was unveiled in June 2010 on the website, YouTube. A Fox News report re-broadcast on the site showed a fourth-grade teacher in Oakland introducing these innocent 8- and 9-year-olds to the concept that they can be either male or female – whichever they choose – just like their friends in the wild-animal world. Of course, this is being done without parental consent. Masqueraded attempts to justify homosexuality to youngsters is bad enough; this is a form of open warfare on God-created sexuality and parental consent and prerogatives. If children are encouraged to believe they are no different from the rest of the animal kingdom, can the mandatory sanctioning of bestiality not be far behind? After all, "gay" marriage has reached that threshold.

Back in Tucson, meanwhile, Mike Shaw told my radio audience, "They tried to teach the 'critical-race' theory 20 or 30 years ago through the filter of race," and that did not work. Today, the same miscreants are advancing "the idea that this was a country (*Aztlan*) invaded by Europeans and that it needs to be re-populated by the *Raza*." Students, he said, "can take (the new agenda) as a U.S. History credit without learning about the U.S. Constitution." Which is about as radical as one can get, save the anti-patriots' idea that the Pilgrims brought disease and that Thanksgiving should instead be a day of atonement.

In fact, according to author Brent Bozell, who heads the Media Research Center, which monitors mass media liberal bias on a daily basis, some of the worst radical minds are at work today as anchors on television network newscasts. One, he said, is Ann Curry, longtime *Today* morning show news-reader on NBC, who in June 2011 was elevated to one of the top two anchor spots before eventually being sacked by the network in 2012, perhaps because management came to realize exactly *how* biased she actually was. Curry, Bozell wrote, was interviewing in 2003 the author of a book urging families to learn more about the history of Thanksgiving and to appreciate being American. Stated Curry, "You know there are some American Indians who feel that Thanksgiving should be a day of mourning, not a day celebration, because of what happened to their people." She must have read one of Howard Zinn's books because this sounded as if were right out of the pages of *A People's History of the United States*.

Also in Arizona, a bill passed in 2010 by the state legislature, which was signed into law by Republican Gov. Jan Brewer, "bans classes in kindergarten through 12th grade that promote the overthrow of the U.S. government, promote resentment toward a race or class of people, (and) are designated primarily for pupils of one ethnic group or advocate ethnic solidarity." Commented Bobby Eberle, founder of *GOPUSA.com*, in reporting this development on his website, "What's utterly amazing is that the law was actually needed in the first place."

As for me, I agree completely with that sentiment, and I firmly believe that, fueled by this evidence, propaganda is rampant in the educational system and not unique to Arizona. This is happening all over the country, just perhaps not to this degree, because left-wing activists are cagey and cautious in nuancing their motives and moves, one step at a time – except when they are violently and publicly protesting *en masse*. The shame in this particular case is that, instead of learning to be literate, the students are being taught to protest.

If one does not subscribe to the idea that machinations promulgated by so-called education reformers are matters of constantly creeping socialism, then consider the comment of a spokeswoman for a food-monitoring group quoted in the wake of the Los Angeles Unified School District's June 2011 ban of flavored milks for its students. This "nutrition Nazi" exulted in the school board's 5-2 decision as a victory for "social justice." Heck with nutrition or any child's well-being but hurray for further advancement of the socialistic agenda. The two dissenters insisted that the move demonized milk and allowed a television chef to dictate how their district operates. The dissenters emphasized that fruit juice advocated by leftist food fetishists has more sugar than flavored milk.

Apparently one does not have to necessarily be a U.S. resident or citizen to foist his or her political and socio-economic philosophy on America's school children. To wit: Jamie Oliver, the British foodie who appears regularly on U.S. television and has endeavored to "revolutionize" children's food and beverage consumption. Oliver was the chef to whom the dissenters on the school board referred. Although a familiar face on U.S. TV screens, he lives not in this country but in his native England. And I thought we rid ourselves of the Brits dictating their whims to us when the Colonists declared independence in 1776.

___

In exhaustive research and interviews for his 90-minute documentary film, *Agenda: Grinding America Down*, Idaho-based Producer/Director/Writer Curtis Bowers lends great credence to the obvious nature of the revisionists' aims.

Buttressing Bowers's findings is conservative Beverly Eakman, an author, reformer and head of the National Education Consortium. Eakman asserts that children already are the first targets of those trying to bring our public-school system to its knees.

"We are losing the majority of our children to the other side," Bowers said, because of constant indoctrination, from kindergarten through 12th grade, and well into college, where tenured Marxist academics hold sway. These campus political operatives have targeted ages 15-25, according to longtime respected anti-feminist Phyllis Schlafly, who said it is done "to get the children to abandon their parents' beliefs" all the way up through postgraduate levels.

In one audience for a showing of Bowers's film, an elderly man stood up during a post-screening question-and-answer period and recounted how a young man at a nearby high school had been punished by school officials for displaying 3-by-5-inch stickers of the American flag on his car windows. He was later exonerated of the "crime" in a letter from a faculty member after his parents and other adult supporters vehemently protested the original decision. When the elderly man was finished, Bowers replied that "diversity was practiced as long as its's not Biblical Christianity," or just old-fashioned American patriotism.

"Social justice" is currently the phrase of choice for radical leftists, yet it is nothing more than a buzzword for socialism, communism or redistribution, not just of income but thought.

The eminent historian, David McCullough, who typically writes fact-based biographies and other books about the American Revolution and our Founding Fathers, has added his name to the growing legions of critics of American education as it now stands. Although he is in his late 70s, McCullough has retained his always keen insights when he observes that textbooks have become "so politically correct as to be comic."

This is nothing, however, because as McCullough told a *Wall Street Journal* interviewer in June 2011, "We're raising young people who are, by and large, historically illiterate," and that he began worrying about it two decades ago, when approached by a college sophomore following an appearance at "a very good university in the Midwest," he told the *Journal* reporter. "I know how much these young people – even at the most esteemed institutions of higher learning – don't know. It's shocking."

While McCullough insists the answer to this dilemma is to teach the subject better, the real answer is manifold: First, go back to the basics in grammar school, including reading, writing and factual accounts of history, then keep the political correctness and social engineering out of the classroom, even as our youths matriculate at the college level.

There are numerous positive examples at the local level where decent people are standing up to demand education reform. I am proud that some of these efforts are occurring in my native Colorado, although some glitches remain.

In my home county, Jefferson, where I have lived most of my adult life, the state's largest school district, a billion-dollar-plus, county-wide bureaucracy, is being challenged by a brave group called Jefferson County Students First. A representative of that group, Kathy Peterson, told an interested audience not long ago that 94 percent of the district's 10th-graders were not proficient in mathematics. So what solution do district administrators offer? Why, English as a Second Language. Talk about officials being tone-deaf. English should be taught from Day One – pre-school, kindergarten, first grade, whatever – as both *the* primary language and official language. Any others should be offered, only much later, as middle-school or high-school electives. (Unfortunately, two liberals were newly elected to the school board in November 2011, thus at least temporarily setting back the potential for quicker progress.)

To further illustrate the asinine philosophy of my home school district, Jefferson County, in October 2011, high-school students innocently wearing T-shirts with "Border Patrol" emblazoned on them were summarily suspended. But instead of owning-up to the onerous deed of cutting off these teen-agers from classes, the district instead tried to deny the action had transpired. In television news reports after the suspensions, I called this a case of political correctness run amok.

Little over an hour's drive north of Jefferson County, in Fort Collins, similar consternation is affecting the populace: Concerned citizens are rising up and actively recruiting conservatives to seek seats on school boards dominated by liberals hand-picked by socialistic teachers' unions. Conservative activist Laurie Marks has described how groups such as Right Turn Colorado are at the forefront of this movement to shake up the traditional education establishment and unions.

In the same city, not far from Laurie Marks's home, my former congressional colleague, Bob Schaffer, reform-minded chairman of the State Board of Education, also is principal of a successful charter high school.

Having been a humble (or not so humble, if you ask my critics) public servant for many years – first as a junior-high history and civics teacher, then later as both an elected and appointed official – I can tell you I have striven to do my part to change the new *status quo*. For instance, I once offered a non-binding resolution in the U.S. House of Representatives that expressed a desire for local school boards to encourage students to demonstrate the ability to articulate an appreciation of "American Exceptionalism." The resolution, which lost, stated that this ability be required for any student to graduate from high school.

Despite its failure in Congress, this is not a futile effort. I am part of a forceful movement to use Colorado as an incubator through Schaffer and the state board. I am confident I am not acting alone or in vain, for a former staffer of mine, Charlcie Russell, who lives in Douglas County, just south of Denver, has a plan to teach the topic

TOM TANCREDO

annually on American Constitution Day, Sept. 17. Furthermore, Russell encourages parents, along with grandparents, aunts and uncles, to approach people they know to seek elective office, not just school-board seats. As Curtis Bowers has said, it is "influencing your family and your own circle of friends."

Individual states have to pass resolutions similar to the one I attempted in the U.S. House, as a part of establishing standards and assessments, but first must be the public's willingness to have decent people elected to school boards and state legislatures. Our solemn responsibility is to bring these issues to the public's attention. Otherwise, this would be an exercise in futility.

Much to its credit, the Colorado House of Representatives, my old *milieu*, passed a resolution the final week of its 2011 session encouraging the State Board of Education to direct state public schools to teach American Exceptionalism. The resolution's prime sponsor, freshman Rep. Chris Holbert, correctly referred to our country as a "representative republic" in which yet another then-fellow GOP freshman, Don Beezley, stated, "We own ourselves."

The only members vocally opposing the Holbert resolution were Democrats, although one lame-duck conservative Democrat, who represented the rural, southeastern corner of Colorado, signed on as a co-sponsor with otherwise-Republican co-sponsors. (Resolutions only can encourage action or signify legislative intent; they are different from regular bills, in which legislative passage can directly lead to enacted state law if signed by the

189

governor.) In the following election, any good by the slim
GOP majority was negated by the Democrats' 2012
victory that resulted in the 2013 legislative session,
coupled with a Democrat governor, and controversial laws
approving in-state tuition for illegal aliens, homosexual
civil unions and stringent, unrealistic gun-control laws.

The battle still remains uphill, however, on other
fronts. In one of the states right next-door to Colorado,
Nebraska, that state's largest school district, Omaha
Public Schools, is using some of Barack Obama's
"Porkulus" money in the name of progressive education.
The *Omaha World-Herald* reported that district has taken
more than $130,000 in so-called stimulus funding "to buy
each teacher, administrator and staff member a manual on
how to become more culturally sensitive." The 11-
member school board unanimously mandated that the
book even be given to custodians (causing me to comment
that maybe voters should instead "clean house" on the
school board). The board believes this latest dissemination
will contribute to ending racism, "recognize historically
oppressed populations of children" and "dismantle
historical forms of oppression (existing) in schools."

Conservative pundit Doug Patton, a longtime
Omaha-area resident, wrote that this is tantamount to
making propaganda mills of the local schools – which it
indeed is. "Is it long past time that we realize that
tomorrow's leaders are in the hands of Marxists who, from
top to bottom, now permeate our education
establishment," Patton opined, emphasizing that it is time

to "rescue them from those who would indoctrinate their minds and crush their spirits."

When today's children, crippled mentally by the current philosophical climate, become "parents," how can they be expected to monitor the next generation? That is a perplexing question to which there is not an easy answer. Textbook publishers give in too readily to the "cult of multiculturalism" in which there are no true moral values. Consequently, what results is a world of myths, urban legends and historical falsehoods, perpetuating themselves from one new generation to the next.

One approach, among others, that seems to work, although it is not perfect, is that of the Texas Textbook Committee, on which sits representatives from every State Board of Education district in Texas. Unlike any other state, Texas has assembled a group of citizens of all races, creeds and political viewpoints to review proposed texts, then vote democratically – amid all the attendant controversy, of course – whether to approve the books, for statewide usage at all levels from kindergarten through 12th grade. In other words, a sixth-grader in El Paso uses the *same* book as a sixth-grader nearly 1,000 miles across the state in Beaumont. Not just in Texas, but any state, this same principle can be used by local school boards. To do so, however, they must recognize the multiplicity of existing problems without letting false "diversity" stand in the way of genuine reforms and ongoing improvements.

Unlike the Texas method, there are less-than-perfect statewide approaches to formulating a so-called universal curriculum, especially in a liberal bastion like Minnesota. In a June 2011 profile of my former U.S. House colleague Michele Bachmann (who dropped her bid for the GOP presidential nod in January 2012), for instance, writer Matthew Continetti detailed what the pitfalls can be:

> In 1998, in order to secure federal education money, he wrote, Minnesota adopted a state curriculum called Profile of Learning (which) ". . . amounted to the bureaucrats writing the lesson plans for teachers," Republican Allen Quist was quoted by Continetti. Also, (Quist was further quoted), "Whoever writes the lesson plans really controls what's being taught." The standards, Continetti wrote, were "shockingly low." How low? he rhetorically asked, then answered his own question: (So low that) one day in the late 1990s, one of Bachmann's foster daughters, then in the eleventh grade, took out her math homework. The assignment was to color it. . . . Not only were the standards poor, the author pointed out, but he said Bachmann "regarded the Profile of Learning as tantamount to brainwashing." Continetti quoted Bachmann further : "What you might call a kind of radical left political indoctrination was coming in that wasn't necessarily reflective of the attitudes, values, and beliefs of parents."

"Historically illiterate American kids typically grow up to be historically illiterate American adults. And Americans' ignorance of history is a familiar tale," columnist Jeff Jacoby wrote in June 2011 in the *Boston Globe*. Jacoby was commenting on results of the latest National Assessment of Educational Progress (NAEP) study, "the Nation's Report Card." It concluded that less than one-fourth of U.S. students is proficient in American history, and the percentage continues to decline. Predictably, similar weaknesses were demonstrated in subjects other than history. Sadly, still, Jacoby noted that when *Newsweek* magazine administered the official U.S. citizenship test to 1,000 Americans in early 2010, the results were not laudatory: 33 percent of respondents did not know when the Declaration of Independence was adopted; 65 percent could not say what happened at the Constitutional Convention; and 80 percent had no idea who was president during World War I.

The bottom line in all this is for us to keep pushing to teach our future adults that this still *is* the greatest country that ever existed.

Despite the mechanical aspects falling far short of even minimal expectations, there is a more heinous danger lurking in our classrooms amid the indoctrination and inculcation of young minds with the constant drumbeat of socialist ideology. It is critical to understand that the incremental revolution from within – rather than the traditional revolution in the streets, as was the case in the turbulent '60s – is what drives the wheel of socialists. If one foot is in the door at a time, then the door keeps opening further until the room that once represented traditional values ultimately is supplanted by this new order. These doors first are entered in the nation's schools.

In the words of Phyllis Schlafly, rather than biology, chemistry and other disciplines being taught, instead we have "the science of victimology." Capitalism, Biblical Christianity and traditional values are the "bullies" (to use a common strategic term employed today with other ulterior motives, tied to the homosexual agenda), and virtually everyone else is a "victim." The left basically opposes morality as we know it, and therefore promulgates a breakdown of cultural traditions, making it easy to sell in an increasingly soulless environment, as Curtis Bowers sees it. But morality is not a tangible; it is simply having the character to do what one *should* do, not what one is *forced* to do.

Here is a more-concrete example: A thing I call the "moral compass" prevents any of us from going out tomorrow and robbing a bank or convenience store. If that compass did not exist inside each of us, we would need a cop on every street corner. Western Civilization has provided more for the world than anything we have ever experienced, yet it is the most degraded institution, beginning in our schools.

This collective brainwashing carries over from schools into the street. Something is dreadfully wrong when thousands of students riot at Penn State after late Coach Joe Paterno gets fired for facilitating the perpetration of pedophilia and child molestation by a trusted longtime assistant coach. That scandal broke in November 2011 amid all the various concurrent fronts of the Occupy movement. In either case, there is an issue of morality, or lack thereof. Yet, what do we expect from a culture that is constantly bombarded with immorality, triggering a moral denigration of human society? We need a moral people for a republic like ours to work. You either are petrified at what you hear (in the mass media) or you are simply mad as hell, like the Peter Finch-portrayed news anchor in the classic movie, *Network.*

I am embarrassed to report that not all is bright in my home state for the immediate future concerning our children and keeping radicals from mandating and dictating their tasteless preferences onto the rest of us. A recent instance was detailed in the *Denver Post* regarding a new law that requires child-care providers to adhere to a draconian set of rules, including that all doll collections represent three races, and that each classroom contain at least 10 visual displays, with two "representing nature realistically" and two "presenting diversity in a positive way."

Another grievous set of circumstances in my native state several years ago hit me like the stone slung by diminutive David when he slew the giant Goliath in the popular Biblical story that illustrates the differences between good and evil, and right and wrong. In February 2006, in the latter part of the decade that I represented Colorado's Sixth Congressional District, a friend, who also was a constituent, told me of his oldest granddaughter, who was a freshman at Overland High School in my district. The teen-ager had been in what was supposed to be a geography class, taught by a left-wing zealot named Jay Bennish.

The young girl would report to my friend and his wife, her grandparents, almost daily, how "Columbus raped the Arawak peoples." When the couple inquired as to why their granddaughter surmised this, she replied she learned it "in Mr. Bennish's class." Moreover, the student apprised Grandma and Grandpa that Bennish fed his unknowing sycophants hearty helpings of anti-George W. Bush rhetoric, regularly comparing the then-president to Adolf Hitler – a convenient ploy by the Left despite *Der Fuhrer's* brand of National Socialism actually representing more an outcropping of extreme left-wing thought than any rightist ideology. The servings of so-called geography, therefore, were accompanied by unappeasing appetizers of anti-Americanism and unjust desserts of radical mind-manipulation.

As an elected representative, and someone fervently interested in such issues as freedom, national security, border integrity and basic truths about our current and former condition as the greatest nation in the history of the world, my interest simultaneously was heightened rather naturally. This was true for more than one reason. First, for years in the North Denver neighborhood in which I was raised – a largely Italian-American enclave where Christopher Columbus was a true hero – American Indian activists and other fellow-travelers instigated protests

196

against the annual Columbus Day Parade each October. Second, the longtime nearby park, which was the area's cultural focus, was named for the great explorer and discoverer of the New World. However, fueled by a combination of activist pressure, political correctness and historical dishonesty, the park's original name was changed to Columbus-La Raza Park. (Considering the certainty and rapidity in effecting the name change, it puzzled me, with my tongue firmly in cheek, that it was not changed instead to "La Raza-Columbus," but the Denver City Council had to throw a bone to the shrinking Italian-American community that still lived near the park.) Third, about the same time my friend's granddaughter was intoning the daily "Arawak" chant, a bold, fearless young male student in one of Jay Bennish's classes was surreptitiously recording some class sessions on a digital audio player. As a former teacher interested in the unvarnished truth, my curiosity, too, was piqued by this aspect.

When the young man turned over his recordings to a nationally syndicated, free-market-oriented columnist and to Colorado's highest-rated AM radio station, Bennish was exposed, not just locally and nationally, but, in this age of global communications, well beyond our own borders. So, what had been a small spark of controversial teaching methods erupted into a raging firestorm. Bennish was ultimately rebuked by the school district and placed on "administrative leave" (another latter-day, politically correct euphemism for suspension) for a short period. It was something akin to "show" trials that despots have conducted over the years to placate critics and accusers.

However, in the long term, Bennish was soon back in the classroom, yet with relatively toned-down rhetoric – for fear, no doubt, that some other courageous student might bring a secret recording device into the room.

(At about the same time the Bennish brouhaha was brewing, in October 2007, my fellow Italian-Americans who organized Denver's Columbus Day parade invited me to be Grand Marshal. I accepted and was standing at the staging point downtown when a plainclothes policeman approached me and asked, "Congressman, are you aware of all the threats on your life TODAY?" I replied, "You mean more than usual?" Then the officer, sober-faced throughout, and perhaps in his own way grasping my feeble attempt at gallows humor associated with being an elected official, matter-of-factly opened a notebook and started reading off a list of people who threatened bomb-throwing and bodily harm once the parade reached the busy spectator viewing point of 15th and Curtis streets. I asked the officer, "Have you arrested them?" Then he replied, "When we got there, they were gone," and he pulled out straps of large, .223-caliber shells, and I reassured him, "Now that you've got my 'attention', what do you want me to do?" The police had arrested 82 protesters, so I told him, "Give me some options," and the officer advised me not to climb aboard the float-like, flatbed truck that bore a sign declaring "Italian-American" and "Republican" on its side; he counseled me further that a police escort would walk with me and be "inconspicuous." "No, I want you to be as *conspicuous* as possible. I don't want to be a hero. I want to make it through this alive," I said.)

(I have been in many parades and usually did not pay much attention, but this time I was aware of everything around me, even people in windows. Finally, as the parade wound down in front of the State Capitol, a young woman, about maybe 16 or 18, dressed in tatters and holding a bunch of rags, made eye contact with me amid Native Americans and others committing disobedient and uncivil acts. The woman stepped off the curb and started moving towards me when a police officer confronted her to ask what were the contents of the bundle. Then she took out a baby, less than a year old, it seemed, held the baby's fingers back, with only the infant's middle finger pointed at me. I immediately thought to myself, "What chance do you think that baby has in life?")

(In a similar vein to the parade incident, one day while I was preparing to leave Washington for a trip to give an anti-illegal immigration speech in Southern California, a Capitol Police supervisor approached me; he said the department's protective services arm was sending escorts for me to ensure my safety amid a potentially hostile situation. I did not know such a division even existed, and the supervisor informed me they NEVER had to do this for any senator or congressman – I was the first, EVER. It sent a chill up my spine, merely thinking that persons so professionally concerned about security on the opposite coast were on alert mode because they *knew* that someone from the civil-disobedience camp was primed to do harm to me or others, simply because these radicals did not share views with us. For me, this was an educational experience in its own right.)

Back to my friend, and his granddaughter, though. Through them, it was learned that Bennish was mandating that students use *A People's History of the United States*, by the late Howard Zinn, as their primary supplemental textbook. If Zinn (whose fallacious arguments were deconstructed in Chapter 1) was the "godfather" of bending history, then his book is the "bible" of this abhorrent movement. As bad as Zinn's ideas are, what is worse is that this man, Howard Zinn, was a U.S. Army Air Corps bombardier, flying many missions over Europe to fight Nazism and Fascism, during World War II. I have often wondered and pondered how the likes of Zinn and film director and Chapter 4 subject Oliver Stone, who fought as a U.S. Marine in Vietnam, could honorably wear the uniform, then take such a severe left turn, and basically betray the country for which they fought by harboring such seditious, yea traitorous, ideas. Furthermore, the Jay Bennishes, and the majority of those in the academic world like him, pollute all these fertile, unsuspecting young minds with an ongoing onslaught of the same false premises.

My constituent friend mentioned here was another mere example; there are literally countless numbers of parents like him and his wife who have seen their children's and grandchildren's morality threatened and emasculated by a reckless and feckless teacher like Jay Bennish in Aurora, Colo.

In Bennish's case, he has insisted that his presentations to students consisted of "both sides." However, as evidenced in the recordings made by the one

young man of real classroom sessions, the ploy Bennish
actually used was to first hammer home his own biases
and mistruths, then "open" the floor to "discussion,"
with the pupils' minds already awash in the singular
viewpoint of Bennish. The disgraced teacher somewhat
reluctantly admitted later under pressure from both
school district officials and the public that this is how it all
occurred. In at least one recording, Bennish, like soulmate
Oliver Stone, made the Bush-Hitler comparison with
characteristic stinging vitriol. Now, I've had my own
legitimate philosophical and political disagreements with
George W. Bush over the years, so much so that I became
persona non grata in the Bush White House, but he is *not*
anywhere close to being a Hitler.

Yet perhaps worse, some of the following
inaccuracies were contained in recorded sessions of
Bennish's comments:

> -- He said that the U.S. was the world's
> largest producer of cigarettes. In fact, China,
> India and Brazil at the time were
> manufacturing more cigarettes than the
> United States.

> -- He claimed that North Carolina was
> responsible for most of U.S. tobacco
> production, but the U.S. Department of
> Agriculture estimated that the state
> contributed only 37 percent of national
> production. Yet North Carolina did produce
> more tobacco than any other state.

-- He stated that "the Israeli-Zionist movement" assassinated the British prime minister in Palestine. The closest individual fitting this description was Lord Moyne, Minister Resident for the Middle East, who was assassinated by Lehi in 1944, a few years before Israel came into existence. The incident would be more accurately described as "*Jewish extremists* assassinated the British minister *responsible for Palestine*".

-- He insisted that the Federal Bureau of Investigation had an office in the World Trade Center, which was not the case. However, the Central Intelligence Agency, the Department of Defense and other U.S. government agencies did have offices there, and former FBI agent John O'Neill was the head of security at the center.

As for my friend and his granddaughter, the girl is now a young woman in her early 20s. Since my friend's oldest daughter, the girl's mother, works full-time days, she gave her retired parents permission to yank the student from public school to home-school her – which they did from her sophomore through senior years. The result: Valedictorian among 15 fellow home-schooled graduates, and a studious, productive, tax-paying adult who cherishes freedom and no longer believes any of the *faux*-history that was forced upon her unsuspectingly as a 15-year-old.

Obviously, "evil profesor" Jay Bennish's Colorado laboratory is not the only locale for experiments in

America-bashing by using radical mind games. Based originally on a report by investigative reporter Eric Stakelback, for CNS TV, that aired in October 2008, and reaffirmed by *Patriot Update* in January 2012, Saudi-funded textbooks were being used in our nation's K-12 classrooms. Among teaching subject matter were that Jesus was a "Palestinian," the state of Israel never existed, Jerusalem is an Arab city and Muslims discovered America before Columbus. At this rate, perhaps even Saudi grade-school textbooks, complete with *jihadi* and *dhimmi* declarations, will come to instruct U.S. school-children, which would be the final nail in the cultural coffin – that is, unless these murderous so-called religionists do not blow us all to bits before then.

A new report by the non-profit Institute for Jewish and Community Research finds that U.S. high-school and elementary textbooks contain countless inaccuracies about Christianity, Judaism, Israel and the Middle East (which BTW has been given the PC name of "Southwest Asia").

On a similar front, the vigilant watchdog group, ACT! for America Education, released in March 2012 results of a textbook analysis report, "Education or Indoctrination? The Treatment of Islam in 6th through 12th Grade American Textbooks," culminating more than three years of planning, research, writing and editing. The 230-page report was "painstakingly researched," according to its publishers, and includes 230 pages, nearly 375 footnotes and 275 bibliography. Some project conclusions include the following:

> "When dealing with the 9/11 terrorist attack, the textbooks routinely omit any reference ... that the terrorists were Muslims or that they were acting in the cause of Islamic *jihad*. Imagine textbooks in 1951 teaching about the attack on Pearl Harbor and neglecting to mention that the attack was perpetrated by the Japanese Imperial Navy."

In a further affront to our moral sensibilities, California (Where else?) in July 2011 is where Governor Jerry Brown signed into law a mandate that public-school textbooks include the accomplishments of homosexual Americans. According to a Bloomberg News report, it made California the first state to require the teaching of homosexual history. The law directs social-science classes to include "the role and contributions of lesbian, gay, bisexual and transgendered people" as well as those with physical or mental disabilities.

It is no surprise, considering the ongoing avalanche of this type of immorality, our most-populous state is bankrupt not only fiscally but morally. One wonders if California textbooks would ever tackle the issue of these various perverse behaviors and orientations as valid forms of mental illness?

Michael Reagan, syndicated radio talk-show host and columnist, and the adopted son of the late, great President Reagan, opined, "When I was a youngster, I was teased and bullied for being an adopted child. In view of my personal experiences, should we add the contributions of adoptees to the legislation? How about adding the contributions of skinny kids, or kids with red hair, or extra-long legs or eyeglasses?"

Like Michael Reagan, I wonder where it will stop. We do not have to wait for further encroachment of gay marriage to have our innocent children involuntarily introduced as early as possible to homosexuality. The Golden State already has won the gold medal for that. I predict that it will not be long before California mandates that textbooks endorse such deviant behaviors as polygamy and polyandry.

In the Bloomberg report, implications for the textbook industry were highlighted because textbook publishers typically try to sell California-approved texts to other states. The Association of American Publishers was quoted as saying that California, as the nation's largest buyer, accounted for almost 13 percent of the $3.4 billion market in 2009.

Then there is the utterly sickening case of the previously mentioned Ward Churchill. This fraud, who was proven to have no Indian blood at all, passed himself off as at least part-Indian for years to advance his standing in professorial circles. His rise culminated in a high-salaried tenured position at the taxpayer-funded University of Colorado at Boulder in the Ethnic Studies Department. However, Churchill's downfall was manifold – he was accused, and found culpable, of "research misconduct" and also of embarrassing the university with his radical protesting activities. The university's Board of Regents dismissed him in 2007 after 17 years on the faculty, and Churchill's attempts to be reinstated via the appeals process eventually were denied.

I had much up-close knowledge of this middle-aged hippie's histrionics during his frequent fights to try and prevent the Columbus Day parade near my old boyhood neighborhood in North Denver, and later when I was president of a think tank, the Independence Institute, which he sometimes criticized for its unbridled mission of advancing liberty and free-market principles.

As documented earlier in this chapter (and photographed by Tucson's Mike Shaw during demonstrations in Arizona), Churchill has reveled in his role as an activist – not unlike Barack Obama before he was an elected official. So-called Native Americans, and other aggrieved ethnic groups, could count on the long-haired Illinois native to show up to encourage various forms of civil disobedience. If one had the misfortune to appear as a debate opponent or on a discussion panel with Churchill, it was assured that, if the fake-Indian was losing his argument, he would shout you down, in typical angry-radical fashion – often with profanity-laced tirades.

Ward Churchill still lingers on the fringes of political activism, but there are numerous "clones" at virtually all U.S. colleges, either as compliant students or complicit faculty members, who additionally have the Internet to spread their vile theories and lies.

In my state, a group of leftist college professors in the fall of 2011, responding to Churchill's fate, issued a manifesto encouraging their colleagues to avoid seeking faculty positions at the University of Colorado. Their faulty rationale was that the institution stifles academic freedom and "free" thinking. Well, in some way, they are correct in that, like on nearly every college campus in America, conservative thought indeed is stymied and stifled by the tenured Marxists who control most department chairmanships.

In spring 2012, a supposedly mature, 50-something leftist, Elizabeth Warren, channeled Churchill – Ward, not Winston – rather immaturely by reiterating her career-long claim of being 1/32 Cherokee Indian. That self-proclaimed drop of Native American blood is unimportant, on the surface. Where it is important, however, is that Warren, the Democrat who in November 2012 was elected to the U.S. Senate in Massachusetts, has, like Ward Churchill, passed herself off as a minority for years – to unfairly gain special faculty status at Harvard Law School and other universities. Immediately prior to successfully challenging Republican incumbent Scott Brown for a full, six-year Senate term, Warren had been rejected by that body as Barack Obama's nominee to head a characteristically unnecessary and bloated new agency, the Consumer Protection Financial Bureau – a proposed entity that had been her personal brainchild. Being a fake Indian, though, it turns out is no deterrent to being elected to the world's most-boring deliberative body.

Collectively, as a society, we must continue to be vigilant and diligent in battling the excesses of socialism and political correctness that attack our nation's young minds on a daily basis. This culture war will not be close to being won until decent, law-abiding, God-fearing citizens form solid majorities on school boards and also in various legislative bodies from local levels up through Congress. Plus, we have to make our voices heard to ensure that courts in every jurisdiction are populated by jurists, whether appointed or elected, who genuinely respect the Constitution and its original intent. The Tea Party "Teanami" that surged ashore in 2010 all over America and picked up momentum in 2012 at least in individual U.S. House races needs to crest even higher in the future.

8

FAMILIAR AND NOT-SO-FAMILIAR FACES, BUT THEY RING THE SAME

There are 435 members of the U.S. House of Representatives. When that body gave authorization for President George W. Bush to commit U.S. forces to Iraq on the heels of the 9-11 attacks in 2001, the resolution passed 434-1. The lone dissenting vote was cast by someone who first was elected to Congress the same year as me in 1998, Rep. Barbara Lee. Although she and I were sworn in on the same day, there is no one with whom I served who could be as diametrically different from me on virtually every issue. If Barbara Lee were a "historian," like, say, Howard Zinn, you might accurately call her the ultimate liberal revisionist. That one vote thrust a relatively obscure, but ultra-liberal, congresswoman into a spotlight she might not normally would have otherwise occupied, or even sought. For her first three years up to that point, Lee seemed content to do the bidding of her very-liberal California district and serve as back-bencher in the radical, all-Democrat Congressional Black Caucus until her elevation to that group's chairmanship, and attendant attention-getting pulpit, several years later.

In order to fully understand Lee, though, you have to realize how her background and life's experiences helped fashion her worldview. Much like Barack Obama, she wrote a 2008 autobiography, *Renegade for Peace & Justice: Congresswoman Barbara Lee Speaks for Me.* In it, she shares the path to radicalization that was shaped by such "liberation theology" preachers as the Rev. Dr. Hazaiah Williams and the Rev Dr. J. Alfred Smith, Sr., who sound eerily like Obama's spiritual mentor of 20 years, Marxist Rev. Jeremiah Wright. Lee described Smith as "fighting shoulder-to-shoulder for social justice." Along the way – as she advanced through the ranks as a campus and community activist, congressional staffer, California state assemblywoman and, for a short tenure, a state senator – she honed her radicalism by associating with the blood-thirsty leadership of the militant Black Panthers, an odd coupling for a self-described pacifist who admits she does not like to be anywhere near a gun.

More recently, Lee threw her support to the Occupy Oakland protesters who were causing havoc and destroying businesses in the largest cities in her district, Oakland and Berkeley. California's Ninth Congressional District is perhaps the nation's most liberal, also being home to the main campus of the University of California, birthplace of the 1960s Free Speech Movement and an ongoing font of radical Marxist practices. Of the latest manifestation, Lee, instead of condemning the Fleabaggers and their anarchistic behavior, excoriated law enforcement for trying to keep order. "I shared my outrage and grave concern about the police brutality in Oakland directly with the mayor. My thoughts go out to the injured ... I strongly support the Occupy movement and continue to stand with the peaceful protesters in this struggle for economic justice and equality," Lee stated in a posting on the liberal *Huffington Post* website, never once expressing even an iota of concern for the brave law-enforcement officers who put their lives on the line daily to protect the freedom of the Fleabaggers to protest. (Speaking of that Oakland mayor, she is Lee's fellow leftist Jean Quan, who, rather than ordering the mob to disperse, went to the sympathetic media and "asked" protesters to "call me," as if she were inviting them to an afternoon tea as opposed to a genuine Tea Party rally.)

If ever there was a member of Congress totally out of step with the average American – especially those who pay taxes – it would be Barbara Lee, whose lone-wolf vote on the Iraq War resolution was not the only instance of such apostasy to the American Way. And she revels in this rebellious voting pattern, which obviously pleases a certain majority in her district but is at odds with much of the rest of the country, let alone advancing a dangerous viewpoint. "I had made other controversial votes like that when the Clinton administration wanted to use force in Kosovo," Lee writes in *Renegade for Peace and Justice*. "Again I was the sole 'no' vote, and I am sure that in the future I will vote for or against a bill that will earn me the enmity of other members of Congress and the public."

This philosophy and conduct is the result of many years as a peace activist who was trained as a social worker, none of which lends surprise as to why Lee, like her ally in the White House, has ended up this way.

Although duly authorized by Congress, the Iraq War resolution, in Lee's mind, gave approval for "the strategically foolhardy invasion of Iraq," fueled solely, she insists, by the lust for oil. This line of thinking pushes aside the more complex reasons why everyone in the U.S. House, except Barbara Lee, voted "yea." Her contention that the Bush Doctrine entailed nation-building and preemptive strikes was greatly overridden by the fact that the resolution was a response to our homeland being viciously attacked, without provocation, by Islamofascists from all over the Middle East.

As for anti-war types' insistence that "the world now knows what's been confirmed: that there was no operational relationship between Saddam Hussein and al-Qaeda" and that no weapons of mass destruction (WMDs) were found, as Lee says, that is wrong. The reason no WMDs were discovered is that they were either destroyed or moved to other countries friendly with Saddam's regime after weapons inspectors had previously detected their presence.

Being inculcated over the years with the radical-revisionist-black liberation-theology type sermons by the likes of Revs. Williams and Smith, it is not unusual for Lee to believe the concept that Jesus was a revolutionary

"who would not accept the *status quo* and that if we are true Christians, our life and work is about
taking on a system fraught with racism, sexism, injustice, and oppression and bringing about change." The roots of Lee's own personal Marxism and ultra-leftist activism, then, lie in this bogus creed about Christ as equated with latter-day revolutionaries.

Despite her self-professed belief in God and in her status as a Christian, Barbara Lee is firmly "pro-choice," as in advocating abortion-on-demand, and steadfastly opposes the value of abstinence-only education – two pillars of liberal orthodoxy. The latter, she contends, "is a policy that sadly has not only proven ineffective in preventing teen pregnancy but also has led to the spread of sexually transmitted diseases, or STDs." I ask, then, what about *true* abstinence and virtue, as opposed to unbridled, "free sex"? For starters, how about leaving "sex education" to parents at home? That, however, would be contrary to the Responsible Education About Life (REAL) Act, which Lee introduced in 2007. She described it as "a bill that would have authorized federal funding for states to offer comprehensive and medically accurate sex education." As for abortion, the whole idea of abortion-on-demand is wrongheaded and immoral; no one has a "right" to such a ghastly procedure, which is nothing more than taking an innocent and defenseless life, which begins at conception. Under the guise of providing a woman merely another choice, the Left uses abortion as a form of population control, such as Communist China's one-child policy. Millions of innocent infants have been literally executed in their mothers' wombs over the years, without a peep of protest from Lee and fellow leftists, who prefer instead to overreact to single evil acts like Newtown in order to clamor for more so-called gun-control laws.

Religion is an intensely personal matter in which the heavy hand of government, especially when it is run by essentially Godless socialists, has no place whatsoever. However, with the shoe on the other foot, left-wingers take a different tack. For example, Rep. Barbara Lee opposed the 2001 Community Solutions Act, which would have simply *allowed*, on a voluntary, not mandated, basis, federal funding of church-run social programs, including worship and religious activities. "I opposed this initiative because I oppose government intrusion into our houses of worship, the corrosion of fundamental constitutional principles, and the use of taxpayer dollars to fund discrimination," Lee writes. Yet her ilk firmly advocates sex education, forcing environmental "voodoo" on unsuspecting students and ensuring those same youth are well-versed on homosexuality and other deviant behaviors – all on the taxpayer dime. Based on some leftist perception of discrimination, Lee does not mind forcing religion-based organizations to kowtow to government coercion. This reminds me of how organized religion is treated in a country like China; certain sects are allowed to practice some form of their faith, only after the central government stamps its *imprimatur*; churches that attempt to operate without the communist rulers' blessing are shut down, or their clergy and followers thrown into jail. She says she works "closely with black churches on voter education, registration, and get-out-the-vote efforts because access to the corridors of power are essential to

214

empowering black communities and bringing about change." Yeah, that is really keeping government out of churches, so long as it suits leftists' needs.

As an apologist for the aforementioned collection of thugs, the Black Panther Party, Lee has considered them nothing more than a benign group of social animals and neighborhood healers. She writes:

> "There is an old collective memory (of them) as gun-wielding men who wore black berets and dressed in military style clothing and advocated violence. What's wrong with this image is that the good work they did and their efforts to help the poor and other disenfranchised minorities gets lost in the fray and has been forgotten with time. Carrying guns was a way for the Panthers and other blacks to protect themselves and members of the community from the racist tactics police used at that time. The Panthers were earnest about addressing community issues, and they offered people reasonable, immediate aid and gave them practical options for their day-to-day survival."

Now, I firmly believe in the Second Amendment and the legal right for citizens to bear arms. However, what Lee is talking about is a racist, private army whose members were known for wantonly executing police officers, or "pigs," to use their chosen vernacular; the sidelights of manning community soup kitchens and doling out "care" packages were hardly the Black Panthers' choices of self-*persona*. As the grandson of Italian immigrants, this would be akin to me being an apologist for *Mafiosi*, who would organize neighborhood clubs and do token charity work, while murdering innocent people, running drugs and conducting prostitution and other forms of illegal racketeering.

Part of the canvas of historical revisionism is the incorrect idea, forever advanced by Lee and like-minded thinkers, which traditional history books taught that the continent of Africa was merely a country. Well, I grew up in Colorado – not that far north from where Lee was schooled in West Texas – at about the same time, and I *always* remember Africa being regarded as a continent. Maybe revisionists are confusing Africa with other "A" entries in the atlas, Australia and Antarctica, which some teachers balked as identifying as continents. Says Lee, "African History was not even taught as a subject," yet I contend that while it may or may not have had a separate syllabus, Africa itself was covered in world history and geography, as were all the other continents. "… When World History was covered in class it was the traditional white, Western European curriculum that was taught, a narrow ethnocentric view of history to say the least," Lee writes. Using my necessary logic from above equating the Black Panthers and the Mafia, maybe I should be asking why Italian History never was taught *per se*. That would be pointless, though, since we are all Americans (no hyphens), period, regardless of where our ancestors came from.

Barbara Lee is taken aback by being termed a radical, despite all her public actions and pronouncements over the years lending credence to the accuracy of that label. Critics intend "to use the word as a slur and an insult," she says. "… If being a radical means someone who works to make liberty and justice for all a reality, then call me a radical. If a radical is a person committed to protecting the planet or wanting every man and woman to have access to good paying union jobs with benefits and want all children to have access to public education, then what is wrong with being a radical?" That definition of a radical, in the words of a self-professed one, says it all; what makes someone *really* a radical, however, is the zeal to revise history to suit one's philosophical bent and, worse, to do it forcibly and without taxpayer consent, yet use redistributed tax money to accomplish the dastardly deeds.

There are others desiring to revise history, sometimes by erasing the documented past, otherwise creating "new" history. Oftentimes, these others are like Rep. Lee – they may not be everyday names, but they possess the ability to fly in the face of reality.

One example is Stephen M. Walt, who, under the flag of *Foreign Policy* magazine, authored an op-ed column that appeared in the *Denver Post* in October 2011. The article, which contained five major points, attempted to debunk the honored and earned tradition of American Exceptionalism, a concept rejected by Barack Hussein Obama. Asked early in his presidency if he believed in the concept, Obama replied, "I believe in

American Exceptionalism the same as a Greek believes in Greek Exceptionalism and a Frenchman believes in French Exceptionalism." Translation: No, the President of the United States does *not* accept such a concept, which was enshrined in our unique Constitution (and underscored by the document's Bill of Rights and the great adjunct statement laid out in the Declaration of Independence).

Ditto for Stephen M. Walt, if his op-ed piece is an indication. Walt breaks his points into what he labels as "myths" that reject American Exceptionalism. "The only thing about this self-congratulatory role is that it is mostly a myth," he writes. Here are Walt's five so-called myths:

-- There is something exceptional about American Exceptionalism;

-- The United States behaves better than other nations do;

-- America's success is due to its special genius;

-- The United States is responsible for most of the good in the world;

-- Good is on our side.

I can tell you that – to paraphrase our Founders – it is self-evident there is indeed something truly exceptional, but not mythical, about this grand and enduring experiment we call America. The self-evidence appeared at the founding as the spirit of the Creator injected itself into the *psyche* of those gallant individuals who were guided by principles such as life, liberty and the pursuit of happiness – unlike any other entity before or since. And *that* is what is meant by American Exceptionalism.

It has been proven over time that this country, contrary to Walt's second myth, does behave better than any other nation on a consistent basis. That, too, is an ingrained part of the Great Experiment and the Exceptionalism. When we send troops abroad, it is not to colonize anyone else, yet it is steered by humanitarian principles, including the thwarting of evil-minded forces in defense of first being attacked, rebuilding of infrastructure and instructing new allies in the ways of freedom. All these notable and inherent features are the benchmarks of better behavior, without projecting any self-righteousness.

Look at all the inventions and great ideas that were germinated by Americans, and it is readily apparent that whatever success we have enjoyed is because of a special genius. Whether it be the incandescent light bulb, nuclear power, polio vaccine, the humble cheeseburger, or even such popular sports as baseball and basketball, it was the result of American genius, either by native-born brains or foreign-born intellectuals who proudly became U.S. citizens. Regarding the sports, I like to cite football as an example; the brand played in some form by the NFL, colleges, high schools and Pop Warner leagues since the 1860s is the real deal – American football. In virtually every other country than ours, what the rest of the world calls "football" is actually soccer, which is embraced largely here by "soccer moms" who lean to the left, knee-jerk-wise, on social issues. I prefer our EXCEPTIONAL version.

When you really give a hard look at our surroundings, the United States *is* responsible for most of the good in the world. Despite our warts, and the incessant barbs and attacks on our way of life, other peoples privately envy us and our deep and profound goodness. One of my former constituents who served overseas during the Vietnam Era told me that the natives of other countries called America "the Land of the Big PX," a place where they all dreamed they could live.

(By the same token, I remember something New Zealander Trevor Loudon, author of *Barack Obama and the Enemies Within*, whom I mentioned earlier, told me in March 2012. He said, since his country does not have a Constitution, First Amendment or Second Amendment, and has only a single house of Parliament, their gun laws are quite different from ours; one can own a firearm only by belonging to a gun club, then is put on a three-year waiting list, and the weapon(s) must be stored at the club rather than remain in the gun owner's possession. So much for freedom and individual rights of self-protection against tyranny. I told Loudon that, if we ever "lost" our cherished freedoms in the United States, I had considered going elsewhere and regarded New Zealand as a viable alternative. After that conversation, I have reconsidered.)

It is not that our beloved country is merely responsible for all that good, but despite Walt's contentions, good genuinely is on our side. The United States was created on the Judeo-Christian premise of God-given rights and existence of a Greater Power to guide us. We are the only nation for which such unique founding documents as ours were formulated and which have enduringly survived.

One final point about Stephen M. Walt: Not only does he clearly demonstrate a revisionist's shame in his Five Myths, but with frequent co-author John Mearsheimer, he has a definite anti-Israel bias. I guess this should be expected, though, since the lone beacon in the Middle East that best reflects our principles is the State of Israel.

Barbara Lee and Stephen Walt may not be the most famous critics of the American experience but they are two of the most virulent, if you assess their status by their own words or actions. Similarly, there are numerous lesser-known, yet, equally heinous practitioners.

For instance, like the varied academic violators we discussed in the chapter immediately preceding this one, there are those who spread their particular venom under the guise of textbooks and study guides. A specific example, for one, is *Teaching for Diversity and Social Justice*, published in 1997. It was edited by three left-wing university "social educators," Maurianne Adams, Lee Anne Bell and Pat Griffin. The volume, presented ostensibly as a sourcebook, contains a detailed outline for teaching everything from combating racism and sexism and even something called heterosexism, to applying social justice and diversity in literally any classroom environment. Their book is a classic example of what has gone totally haywire in American education the past two or three decades. The three Rs to these folks are more likely Racism, Reflection and Revision.

Another category of liberal revisionism occurs in books in which non-revisionists have basically been co-opted by allowing their misguided philosophical opposites to share space with them, the idea being to present supposedly balanced viewpoints. The problem with this is it lends validity to the revisionists' argument.

Characteristic of the space-sharing book approach is *The Terrorist Attack on America*, part of the *Current Controversies* series, and published in 2003 by left-leaning Greenhaven Press. The publisher preaches "presenting divergent points of view," which is sort of code for liberal organizations, since it echoes the same tripe as which exists on such outlets as National Public Radio and public television. While the *Terrorist Attack* book includes chapter essays from the likes of conservative writers Don Feder, Bernard Lewis and Mona Charen, plus anti-illegal immigration expert James H. Walsh and my former House colleague Lamar Smith, it is almost overly counter-balanced by the presence of lefty whackos. Blatant examples are Howard Zinn and Noam Chomsky (on whom the first two chapters of this book respectively cast a revealing microscope), Democrat former Colorado Sen. Gary Hart, anti-American writer/activist Larry Everest, the notorious shakedown artist Rev. Jesse Jackson and University of Wisconsin environmental studies professor Rob Nixon. Predictably, and quite incorrectly, the general tack of the liberal essays that assess the post-9/11 landscape is to blame America – and *anybody* but the Islamofascists who actually perpetrated the acts – for the terrorism.

Another manner in which revisionism seeps into our collective minds is via non-fiction works that typically carry titles beginning with "What If ...". These tomes indulge in wholesale speculation of how the world might have been if important events, like wars and political assassinations, had turned out differently. These works should be designated as fiction, or perhaps science fiction, because they tend to make readers believe they are, or could be, true.

Two history professors, Dennis E. Showalter and Harold C. Deutsch, edited *If the Allies Had Fallen: Sixty Alternate Scenarios of World War II*. The book, originally published in 1997 and updated in 2010, winds up concluding that if Axis forces had changed strategies at key junctures during the war, the ultimate result would have been not only German domination but resurgence of the Nazis' erstwhile foe, the Soviet Union. As a true student of history, I find all this fascinating. However, it also is disturbing – for reasons cited above – especially in light of the way history already is mangled in today's schools. It would not be a problem if it were clearly labeled as fiction, but to pass off these musings as fact is dishonest and a danger to the gullible minds that predominate today in Low-Information America.

In the same light is *What If?: Eminent Historians Imagine What Might Have Been.* Rather than focusing on a single conflict such as World War II, Editor Robert Cowley has really challenged documented history, going back to the times of Socrates and Christ, then progressing forward in presenting fictitious musings as if they were hard-rock fact. In *What If?*, published in 2001, Cowley relies quite a bit on outspoken liberal writers who have masqueraded as objective journalists over the years, namely former *Time* magazine essayist Lance Morrow and the late longtime *New York Times* reporter Tom Wicker, who died in late 2011. Similar to the approach used in *If the Allies Had Fallen*, the editor has thrown an occasional bone to a conservative author such as historian/pundit Victor Davis Hanson in order to try and legitimize an otherwise-fallacious effort.

One does not have to be well-known to revise history. The danger lies not in the renown of the revisionist but in the fact that a valid account of the past is susceptible to some disingenuous leftist warping it, then presenting it without admitting the latter's version is fiction, whether it is Barbara Lee, Stephen Walt or whomever.

9
ROBBING PETER TO PAY PAUL;
YOU CAN COUNT ON PAUL'S VOTE

Sometime during his failed quest for the presidency and vice presidency in 2004 and 2008, discredited Democrat former U.S. Sen. John Edwards tried his best to convince voters that there were "Two Americas." One America was populated by the very rich; the rest of America was everybody else, not unlike the inaccurate picture painted by the more recent Occupy movement in its various manifestations. A year-long study of poor families by The Heritage Foundation in 2011 concluded that, from a material standpoint, few Americans were wallowing in poverty, as Edwards and the Flea Party activists implied with their conscious attempts to revise history and propel this country farther down the road to Marxism. Survey results showed that more than 60 percent of all U.S. households, unlike Third World countries, had a conventional oven, microwave oven, refrigerator, more than one television set with cable or satellite, air conditioning, some form of central heating, computer, clothes washer and at least one VCR and DVD player –

not exactly the portrait of poverty. Moreover, the study revealed, among other amenities in poor U.S. households included cordless and cell phones, ceiling fans, clothes dryers, non-portable stereos, coffeemakers, dishwashers and Jacuzzis.

A Gallup Poll for which results were released just after Christmas 2011showed that fewer Americans were less likely to see U.S. society divided into "haves" and "have nots" in any regard, contrary to John Edwards's contentions. The poll compared Americans' opinions to their plight in 2008 and indicated that 58 percent did not think of the country in such a manner, as opposed to 49 percent three years earlier. Like their perennial candidate Edwards, Democrats who were polled by Gallup were the least optimistic, polling at 49 percent in 2011, or nine points less than the average American. As Indiana Gov. Mitch Daniels made clear in the Republican response to President Obama's State of the Union message in January 2012, I, too, prefer to look upon America always as a land of "haves" and "soon to haves."

I have given much thought to the idea of Two Americas, in light of the divisiveness that gripped the nation not long ago, transcending from the sports world even to those not particularly interested in football, regarding former Denver Broncos *wunderkind* quarterback Tim Tebow. It seems people not only in America, but in other countries, lined up on opposing sides because of Tebow's open, yet sincere, professions of faith and religiosity. In the United States, the phenomenon called Tebowmania underscored that, in some way, shape or form, there are indeed two Americas, but it is not like the type envisioned by liberal trial lawyer John Edwards or the Occupy Fleabagger crowd. Using the Tebow example, you might say he became the most influential Christian in the nation, basically with believers squarely on one side of the spectrum and non-believers or lukewarm believers on the opposite flank. This spilled over even into my Denver-area home – our grandchildren wanted Tebow No. 15 jerseys as Christmas presents in 2011, but we could not find any because they were sold out, not just in Colorado but all over the country, including on the Internet. Tim Tebow is reviled by the "anti's" not because of his physical prowess and unorthodox passing style, yet due to the fact he is a Christian and for what he represents on stands he takes.

In December 2011, I "tweeted" a Twitter message asking if anyone would contribute to a fund to construct a Tebow statue. I also asked if I should petition the Catholic Church for possible sainthood for Tebow. Then, when I realized the church requires at least three miracles merely for consideration to be beatified as the first step en route to canonization, I said to myself, "Tebow has already performed seven." (Obviously, Broncos management did not agree with the Tebow-for-sainthood equation, having signed certain future Hall of Fame Quarterback Peyton Manning in March 2012, ostensibly to replace the left-handed phenom, the latter whom they soon afterward traded to the New York Jets with a seventh-round future draft choice in exchange for fourth- and sixth-round draft picks. Then the Jets waived him in the 2013 offseason, and not long afterward Tebow was signed by the New England

Patriots. New England owner Robert Kraft, an observant Jew, acknowledged that he wants players with character like Tebow's on his roster.)

The eminent 19th-century philosopher Friedrich Nietzsche, ironically not a religious man himself, once opined, "I wondered why I hate this man so much, then I remembered why: He's a better man than I am." Could it be that, despite his modesty, humility, fealty to the Lord and willingness to give credit to anybody else but himself, someone like Tim Tebow is a better man than most of the rest of us, even as young man in his mid-20s? He lent great credence to this in his first press conference as a Jet, where he thanked the Broncos and spoke only glowingly of his former team's management despite the somewhat-shabby way he had been discarded by the Denver squad.

Despite the dearth of jerseys – or maybe because of it – I am proud that my grandchildren have seen the goodness to voluntarily select Tim Tebow as a role model. Their prudent judgment, even in their youth, starkly contrasts with that of an adult caller to a Denver radio talk show who, with a hint of hatefulness in his voice, said he would choose a certain rock star over Tebow as a role model for his kids. That same animosity reminds me of the bumper stickers that proclaim: "My child is an honor student at X school." Based on society's sinking *morés*, a newer, counteractive sticker has emerged; it generally reads something like this: "My Labrador retriever is smarter than your honor student," reflecting the kind of banality and intellectual illiteracy and dishonesty of the radio caller and Low-Information America.

In the week after Christmas 2011, I was fill-in co-host of a popular daily radio talk show in Denver. We discussed the moral relativism associated with the pre-Noel mob that stormed a store at an Indianapolis shopping mall to buy limited-edition $180 "retro" Nike Air Jordan basketball shoes. My fellow conservative co-host concluded that, had the crowd been, say, upscale white youths, rather than a predominantly black group, perhaps they might have prized something more like a luxury car rather than mere shoes that were coveted by a less-fortunate demographic. I responded with my own personal anecdote of a trip to supposedly free, post-Soviet Russia where I encountered people in a long queue outside a store to buy basic grocery items; working the line were young entrepreneurs selling black-market shoes – which had nothing to do with eating a square meal but everything to do with status in this topsy-turvy, morally ambiguous world.

It seems that we are approaching a day, as Christians, or believers, where the voracious "beast" of a secular society will force us to congregate in darkened caves to worship similar to the way early Christians gathered in catacombs in ancient Rome.

I also have seriously contemplated an America in which the social engineers who increasingly have taken hostage of our collective souls and minds would set aside various parts of the country where they would "kidnap" our bodies as well, forcing us to live in designated regions. While some of this already has happened in a *de facto* manner, the *de jure* aspect of "assigned living zones" is scary but not totally unrealistic, if Marxist types continue to prevail, with them even feeling the renewed boldness to assess new taxes and fees as a perverse way to gain more votes and added power over the "grateful" *bourgeois* masses.

I call this "robbing Peter to pay Paul," because you then can always count on Paul's vote. Think of a massive welfare state, not unlike what communists have created around the world in the last 100 years or so, where involuntary confiscation of producers' money (Peter's Pence, if you will), earned according to their ability, results in redistribution to takers (the Pauls), according to their need. In polite circles, this is known by more accurate terms, such as extortion and robbery; only in this case the statists who run the country are the criminals. Until recently, for the past four years, we already have had an admitted tax cheat, Timothy Geithner, with a firm grip on the national safe-lock as Obama's secretary of the Treasury, so it would mean not having to travel much farther to achieve this condition. Then there is Democrat former U.S. Sen. and New Jersey Gov. Jon Corzine, chief executive of bankrupt MF Global, who, with remarkably little emotion on his face, told a congressional committee in early 2012 that he had no idea where a missing $1 billion-plus of investors' money went. In March 2012, it was reported that Corzine, while still heading MF Global, had authorized $2 million in questionable money transfers. But the *New York Times,* the so-called "newspaper of record," as it does with most liberals, provided cover for Corzine. Moreover, then, in November 2012, congressional investigators concluded that he indeed was responsible for the missing-funds mystery. However, since there is systemic media bias, created by shameless arrogance and outright cheerleading for leftist pols and their enablers, I am not confident Corzine will ever be prosecuted, and he has managed to walk scot-free as this is written. Ninety percent of Americans get their "news" from this Lamestream Media.

    As for the assigned living zones, the way the country currently is aligned sets the stage for the statists to perform such legerdemain. I mean, the latest presidential election underscored that we already are severely divided by either Red and Blue states, and the poison pen with which Democrat elected officials, and their black-robed allies on the bench, redrew gerrymandered congressional and legislative districts in 2012 is stunningly shocking. If we ever were rounded up according to political philosophies and herded into various places not necessarily of our own choosing, both the East and West coasts would be reserved for liberals and socialists, with the Rust Belt cities of the Great Lakes Region thrown in. This additional territory would stretch from the Twin Cities on the west to Buffalo on the east and would include Milwaukee, Chicago, Detroit and Cleveland, all cities run into the ground over the years by traditional Democrat, and corrupt (oops, I repeat myself), political machines. Most of the rest of the Lower 48 – Flyover Country and much of the Gulf Coast – would be assigned for conservatives. Under this plan, actually, *no one* need relocate because America already is situated as such. Hawaii, as it is today, most likely would be another throw-in to the liberal preserves, whereas Alaska probably would be the final refuge for conservatives. The last location would be appropriate because leftist radicals for years have contended that conservatives have cold hearts, so, using their logic, why not relegate us to one of the world's most-frigid places.

There is a solid case for letting at least one state sort of drift out to sea and never come back since its economy, despite liberals' continual attempts to destroy it, is the world's sixth-largest, so purportedly it could survive on its own without inflicting further ills on the rest of the republic. In his late-1960s book, *The Last Days of the Late, Great State of California*, Curt Gentry provided a prescient precursor scenario of this, using as metaphor a massive earthquake that literally broke off the Golden State into the Pacific. Gentry posited the giant temblor as a literary device to illustrate economic, moral and social decay that already was occurring in our most-populous state; California unfortunately almost always has served as a bellwether for others in the country and world in advancing liberal ideas via Hollywood and the music industry.

More recently – in December 2011 – nationally syndicated conservative radio talk-show host and former San Diego Mayor Roger Hedgecock wrote that the California Dream would become a nightmare for the rest of country if Barack Obama were elected to a second term. Well, Roger, welcome to the next four years of our National Nightmare. Hedgecock's basis was in his day-to-day existence as a California native who has had to endure the effects of the Left's slings and arrows. "If you were wondering what living in Obama's second term would be like, wonder no longer. We in California are living there now," he offered, not long before California voters in November 2012 approved *even more* tax increases, thus accelerating that state's death spiral even further.

Here is some of Hedgecock's evidence:

-- California is essentially a one-party state, even though there have been such Republican governors as Ronald Reagan, George Deukmejian and Pete Wilson over the past half-century or so. What Hedgecock described as a "virulent Democratic Left" has had a prolonged stranglehold on both houses of the legislature and most statewide constitutional offices. This, he stated, was "enabled by a complicit media where every agency of local, county, and state government is run by the public employee unions. The unemployment rate is 12 percent."

--The Golden State has more food-stamp recipients than any other state, and its "Medi-Cal" program for the indigent, a substitute for Medicaid, is much more generous with redistribution of taxpayer dollars than its federal cousin.

--The administrator-to-pupil ratio in California's K-12 schools is among the nation's highest and, even though classes are relatively small, the record amounts of tax money thrown at schools has not help to improve low test scores and increasing dropout rates. (This would be even worse had it not been for Proposition 13, the landmark property-tax limitation that voters approved in 1978.)

-- California has seven income-tax brackets. The top rate is 9.3 percent, which applies to anyone making at least $47,056, hardly a rich person. Then, according to Hedgecock, is the "millionaires' and billionaires'" surcharge of 10.3 percent for incomes of more than $1 million.

-- If that odious income tax is not enough, Edmund G. "Jerry" Brown, Jr., the current and former governor, proposed adding another 2 percent for incomes exceeding $250,000, but even worse for some successful producers, a million-dollar income would then be taxed at 12.3 percent – in *state* taxes alone. Governor "Moonbeam," as he has been popularly known, going back to his first tenure from 1975-1983, also has proposed other increases for beleaguered taxpayers in the insolvent state. "At least five other ballot measures to raise taxes (were) circulating to get on the 2012 ballot in California," the former San Diego mayor wrote. Shockingly, "the (Democrat) governor's proposals (were) the most conservative." (These proposed measures formed the centerpiece of new tax-strangulation laws California's mind-numbed voters rubber-stamped on Nov. 6, 2012.)

-- Hedgecock reported that "the Obama way doesn't end with taxes." An entity called the California High Speed Rail Authority is lording over plans to build a high-speed train connecting Los Angeles and San Francisco. The voters, for whatever reason, approved this fiasco, yet the budget already has exceeded the original estimate by three times. Despite the bloated budget, "the first segment will only connect two small towns in the agricultural Central Valley," the San Diego talk-show host wrote. In the latest development on this issue, a compliant liberal judge in November 2012 struck down a protest of the boondoggle by several owners of prime farmland would food-producing property would be adversely affected.

-- Other beyond-the-pale excesses cited by Hedgecock that have hit well-intentioned California taxpayers hard in the pocketbook – with continual sucker punches to the solar plexus to boot – include radical environmentalism run rampant, overly generous and unnecessary welfare programs and in the topic area so near to *my* heart, immigration abuse. Bottom line for Roger Hedgecock, in warning other Americans

about what could likely happen to them, if
these excesses are not reined in soon at
the ballot box, "It was said after California's
Proposition 13 ... cut property tax rates and
was copied in other states, that whatever
happened in California would soon happen in
your state. You'd better hope that's wrong."

I fear that the breakneck speed at which California
is careening will continue to be duplicated on the federal
level with Obama steering the runaway, high-speed train.

Rather than hold up California as an exemplar of
style and trends, we need to look instead at that state as an
example of what *not* to do with federal funding – whether
regarding the environment, taxes, education, welfare or
border and security issues. Right now, the figurative
"Paul" I mentioned most likely already resides in
California. Although "Peter" populates the rest of the
country, or the *other* America, he has increasingly
discovered what it is like to pay Paul, regardless of the
involuntary confiscatory nature of the payments. Maybe
that readily explains the firestorm of secession petitions
from as many as 40 states that have been posted on the
Internet since the 2012 election.

10

A LIGHTHOUSE OF HOPE

Amid all the darkness of the radicals who threaten our very being, and shining brightly like a beacon at the entrance to the harbor of hope, freedom and liberty, is author/historian Thomas G. West. In his 1997 book, *Vindicating the Founders: Race. Sex, Class, and Justice in the Origins of America,* West forcefully and successfully proves on point after point that the country's Founders were indeed right.

West categorically faces down the radical elements who over the years have sought to tear down the country and re-fashion it in their own mostly Marxist-leaning ways. On each controversial issue – slavery, property rights, suffrage, the family, poverty, welfare – the conservative social scientist has fought back to deconstruct the faulty arguments of the anti-patriots, and he uses the prescient courage of the Founders themselves to counter-punch with aplomb. Frankly, there are few areas on which I find disagreement with West, who proves without much doubt that the Founders' intent was pure and hopeful.

Right from the beginning, West debunks the "anti's" more than adequately. Radicals make three major claims regarding slavery: 1. The Founders never really believed all men were created equal; 2. They did not know the meaning of "created equal"; 3. They knew, full well, what they meant but betrayed their principles with open eyes. West correctly shows all three claims to be false, although he wrestles philosophically in countering No. 3. On No. 1, critics of the Founders continually apply the idea of legal rights, or those favored by law, vs. God-given, "inalienable" rights, the latter which cannot be taken away by *any* government. West easily refutes No. 2, stating, "We can say with confidence, first, that the Founders believed that blacks (despite the original three-fifths provision in the founding documents) are fully human and, second, they knew well what this meant: Slavery in every form violates the right to liberty." However, West surmises, No. 3 is more difficult to refute. Even so, it can be countered because, as time progressed, there were numerous attempts to abolish slavery – starting with limiting slave trade, followed by a state-by-state abolition, since the practice was regulated by the states. In states where slavery remained legal, West insists accurately that it was the doctrines of the American Revolution that led to eventual reforms recognizing slaves' humanity, notwithstanding the Civil War and its role in ending slavery. Among additional reforms West cites were limitations leading to eventual outlawing of importation of humans from abroad; making regulatory laws more humane; and individual slave owners ultimately freeing thousands of slaves.

Anyone who has accurately interpreted the founding documents – from the U.S. Constitution to the Declaration of Independence to the Federalist Papers – can easily conclude how much on target West is regarding slavery and the other key issues. All one has to do is read what each of the major Founders expressed: Washington wanted abolition; John Adams termed slavery "an abhorrence"; Franklin called the practice "an atrocious debasement of human nature"; Hamilton regarded slavery as contrary to the "gift" to all humans "by the laws of God and nature"; and John Jay said the practice was "inconsistent and unjust."

Even Thomas Jefferson, who had reputedly fathered children with some of his slaves, wrote in a letter in his later years that while he doubted the mental abilities of blacks, it did not affect his view of their rights as human beings, according to West. The letter stated the following:

> "Be assured that no person living wishes more sincerely than I do, to see a complete refutation of the doubts. I have myself entertained and expressed on the grade of understanding allotted to them by nature, and to find that in this respect they are on a par with ourselves. ... (B)ut *whatever may be the degree of talent it is no measure of their rights. Because Sir Isaac Newton was superior to others in understanding, he was not therefore lord of the person or property of others*".

The flip-side of slavery was a property issue, West writes, because by definition, slavery takes the property of another without his consent. In other words, any human's physical presence belongs to no one but himself. As then-Colorado Republican state Rep. Don Beezley aptly put it, during a 2011floor debate in my home state's House of Representatives on an American Exceptionalism resolution, "We own ourselves."

David Barton, a respected author and historian who founded and heads a group called Wallbuilders, calls the attempts "over the past 60 years" by radicals to dismantle documented history and highlight all the negatives, "deconstructionism." This is something with which West concurs, in his own way, writing, for instance, that "textbooks are virtually silent on the substantial abolition movement (especially among individuals in the South, leading to the above-mentioned freedom for literally thousands of slaves). Although no Southern state abolished slavery, there was a broad agreement that slavery was wrong," harkening back to the Founders' original intent – a point forever contested by radical critics. In light of all this, it is a gross exaggeration to describe the evolution of the horrendous practice of slavery into permanent abolition as "the unfree origins of the United States."

There is a popular view, promulgated by many so-called historians, such as Paul Finkelman, that implies it was a *Negro* slavery problem by itself confronting the

1781 Constitutional Convention. That view was narrow and shortsighted, as West contends. The threat posed by slavery in any manner was one to *all* citizens. The truth is, slavery took so many years to develop, it would realistically take a number of years to abolish. Finkelman and his like-minded thinkers, West writes, did not consider context. In the long term, slavery was bound to continue – with the Constitution or without. If liberty *for anyone* was to have a future in the newly created republic called America, the indispensable first step was a stronger national government on a democratic basis, buffered by 10th Amendment principles of sovereignty.

West rebuffs three major points of contention by Founders critic Kenneth Karst. First, West emphasizes that it is wrong to use the term "non-whites," as Karst does, in analyzing the Three-Fifths application for slaves, since many blacks were not slaves. Moreover, it was Southerners, *not* Northerners, who said slaves should "stand on an equality with the whites." Second, a clause evolved outside the Constitution in the early 19th century that laid "the foundation for banishing slavery out of this country." Third, West claims that clause was misinterpreted because, although it directed runaway slaves to be returned to their owners, "the language adopted was meant to show no approval of slavery but only an acknowledgement that it exists, and will, for the time being."

"The original intent of the Constitution . . . cannot be understood from its text alone," West explains. Again, this is a question of context, the main point being the

241

Founders were a group of statesmen who generally agreed on the principles of government.

One critic whom West takes to task for gross misinterpretation was prominent 1960s and 1970s civil rights activist Ralph Abernathy, who had been a close confidant of the Rev. Martin Luther King, Jr. The late Abernathy wrote the following (which West includes in his book):

> "There can be no pure memory of an American Revolution that published a declaration that liberty was a right accorded to 'all men' and then created a Constitution that specifically prohibited blacks from enjoying that right. The only logical conclusion that modern blacks can draw from such circumstances is that their forefathers were not regarded as 'men' by the white founders of this country."

Abernathy's thoughts mirror those of what West regards as the "totalitarian impulse at work in Marxist Communism is the imprudent, immoderate and, therefore, immoral demand for the abolition of human evil on earth." This theory, accompanied by the typical impatience and shrillness of the Left, has fueled both the mid-1800s abolition movement and today's leftist revisionism.

Radical left-wingers always have insisted that uncompromising opposition to slavery was the *only* moral course of action, period. West uses a passage from Donald Robinson, author of *Slavery in the Structure of American Politics*, to refute this. Robinson wrote:

> "It is probably fortunate that abolitionism as a movement of consequence in America was still far off in the future, for if Samuel Adams and John Jay and Benjamin Franklin and other Northern politicians had forthrightly criticized slavery in the early 1770s, American history would have developed far differently. To begin with, there would have been no Association of Twelve Colonies in 1774, and certainly no 'Unanimous Declaration of the Thirteen United States of America'."

People are imperfect, West reasons, so there is no perfect solution. For example, he concludes, "This happens every day in small ways. Most Americans believe that cruelty is wrong. Yet most of us have been cruel on many occasions to people we do not like. Sometimes we regret it and feel guilty more often. We barely notice (emancipation vs. selfishness)."

Even political scientist Herbert Storing, who generally defends the Founders, is critical of them for allowing "a large opening toward slavery." While West initially concedes that "opening," he nonetheless says it is wrong (which it is indeed) to criticize the Founders on that account because it is "a genuine, not a fake, moral dilemma," which required prudence and patience to resolve.

Ultimately, states West, "Lincoln was right and today's consensus is wrong. America really was 'conceived in liberty, and dedicated to the proposition that all men are created equal" because blacks over time won more liberty, became equal citizens, gained the right to vote, and eventually had their life, liberty and property equally protected by law. "But today, the founding, which has made all of this possible, is denounced as unjust and anti-black. Surely that uncharitable verdict needs to be reversed." That is one of our constant goals, if we all remain diligent.

On the topic of private property, widespread claims among 20th-century scholars are a constant drumbeat that the Founders effectively had no interest in it. I fervently believe this to be false, and my feelings are echoed by West. He firmly asserts that "nothing could be further from the truth than these claims" and that the documents of the founding era "frequently asserted that property was a fundamental natural right." Without private property, he continues, "government would own churches, printing presses and factories." For instance, government today already owns all rights to electronic broadcasting and can, and has, shut down several radio and television stations "whose broadcast content was judged politically incorrect."

Denouncing of property rights by modern scholars in textbooks is subtle but done by criticizing capitalism and free markets as they evolved later in American history. West states the many charges against so-called "robber barons" of the late 19th century are untrue (as I emphasized in an earlier chapter), and that evidence has shown that the leading businessmen of that era committed few of the injustices attributed to them. However, like today's radicals, who are inherently anti-business, anti-profit and pro-government, these critics found that it was instructive to throw "mud" constantly against the wall, knowing full well that the general, and gullible, public will eventually believe lies, if they are repeated often enough. To paraphrase what Mark Twain famously said, "A lie can travel around the world several times before the truth gets legs."

More recently, hostility toward property rights is apparent in textbooks, such as popularization of the term "Decade of Greed" by Democrats and their media sympathizers in criticism of the Reagan administration, "which promoted property rights through tax (rate) cuts and deregulation," West writes.

West refers to John Locke's *Second Treatise of Government, Chapter 5* to drive home his point about private property correctly being a natural extension of human yearning and the desire for self-achieved freedom, as opposed to the heinous, unnatural act of government as landlord. Locke reasons:

"Man (by being master of himself, and
proprietor of his own person and the
actions or labor of it) had still in himself the
great foundation of property, . . . Thus labor,
in the beginning, gave a right of property
whenever anyone was pleased to employ it
upon what was common."

Locke's logic argues that even as property is
naturally divided or subdivided, it provides further
opportunity for all, but without government coercion.
When I was a congressman and traveled the Sixth District,
I developed a theory that there was, on one hand, an
owner's mentality and, conversely, a renter's mentality.
Typically, owners – whether of homes or businesses –
automatically take pride in that in which they have
invested, whereas renters may not have that pride of
ownership. Yet, one does not need to be an owner *per se*
to possess the owner's mentality, for as I traversed the
district, I noticed there always were those in rental-only
communities, or others who owned a business but leased
the property from someone else, who nonetheless
exhibited such a noble mindset.

The unequal results of equal rights, West states, will
be not only tolerable but just – yet only as long as the right
to acquire is effectually guaranteed to the poor, so that
they can earn enough to buy what they need from this
"common stock." . . . "The majority of today's scholars
are oblivious to the Founders' interest in enabling the poor
to acquire property of their own," he explains. Therefore,
rather than forced redistribution of land holdings to the

246

poor being the natural consequence of the Founders' thinking, it is quite to the contrary. Rather than a device to keep the poor down, the right to acquire property "was understood by the Founders . . . as a protection to rich and poor alike. . . . We implicitly, but not usually explicitly, understand property rights to include the right of *any* citizen to acquire property through his productive efforts, and to use and keep what he earns."

Three leading, and bogus, arguments against property rights have been advanced in the 20th and 21st centuries: 1. It is denied that there is a fundamental right to acquire and possess property; 2. Private ownership of property was no longer regarded as an adequate way to promote economic growth; and 3. Private property is said to be corrupting.

West effectively counters all three arguments: 1. The new view of rights (the former constitutional) distinction between state and society, public and private . . . as long as anyone is in want, the government has a right and, if it is feasible, a duty to intervene and supply the need. (This radical theory is contrary to God-given rights enshrined in the Constitution.); 2. The Founders responded to claims against property rights by defending what West terms "the right above all because it is just, because it is part of liberty, and because it is an indispensable condition of free government"; and 3. Today's theorists reckon that money and greed corrupt property ownership (but in actuality) "property rights promote public as well as private virtues (leading to) substantial wealth, a major component of national strength" in addition to a further reckoning that "national wealth is a condition of national greatness as well as independence . . . a regime of property rights . . . may promote public and private virtue more successfully than any alternative."

If you think leftist radicals have warped ideas about slavery and property rights, consider their feelings toward the Founders regarding women's rights, including the right to vote. According to West, radical feminists ("Feminazis," as I prefer to call them) are not alone in deploring "the Founders' supposed indifference to women's rights" in some revisionist historians' advocacy of retroactively creating a parallel alternative Declaration of Independence that incorporates women's private and public demands. This misses the point, West argues, because similar to other issues, the Founders anticipated eventual changes with implications that all men, and women, were created equal. I agree with him that equality evolved with changing circumstances such as increased longevity, smaller families and women being able to have careers outside of being homemakers.

Major recognition by the Founders highlighted by West involves the inherent differences between men and women, most notably the critical distinction between natural equality and ideological equality. Among other things, he notes physical contrasts between the sexes. But he also promotes the good of the traditional family vs. "alternatives," the latter which basically amounts to deterioration of the family structure to enable more need for government injection. West's reasoning is that, as the

Founders implied, the family is the best route for all -- for legislative, moral and social reasons. In what he calls "republicanizing (small R) the family," West contends that "the Founders' understanding of the family had (such a dramatic effect) that included allowing cruelty as grounds for divorce, a previously unheard-of concept." The decline of the family over the years, he says, has led to a degradation of women. So ultimately, the Founders realized that for marriage to endure and succeed, it involved mutual concessions, yet maintaining courtship and traditional wedlock, as opposed to "transitory" relationships. We see where the radicals' view of "marriage" has gotten us today – a world rife with government-sanctioned homosexual couplings (pun intended), single motherhood with children born out of wedlock, more welfare recipients and a consequent injection of government into private lives.

Property qualifications for voter eligibility varied from state to state in the very early days of our republic. However, most states limited the franchise to adult males, which, again, is misleading, and a point which is used by critics unfairly to excoriate the Founders. It is precisely *because* of the foresightedness of the Founders, that what ultimately evolved – albeit all too slowly -- was full voting rights for all adult citizens. Simultaneously, the United States grew into the wealthiest nation in world history, with a great degree of poverty conquered, West writes, "because the poor were persuaded that protection of property holders would secure their own rights – and their children's – to acquire property of their own." In other words, the most-concrete way to ensure true equality for all is, and always has been, offering every legal citizen the same opportunity, not encouraging government to create "opportunities" and outcomes.

Welfare – and its inevitable connection to poverty -- is another issue that has been misappropriated by the radical Left, which uses it at every turn to slam the Founders. Yet, if the Founders were so wrong, then why have there only been two basic phases to welfare policy in the 230-plus years of this country, as West accurately states? The first phase was from the founding and lasted through "The War on Poverty" in 1965, nearly two centuries later; the second phase has encompassed welfare policy since then – which clearly offers an explanation as to why things have gone downhill, and continue to spiral downward so rapidly.

Most accounts of poverty have concluded that nothing was done about it until about 1900, with the advent of muckraking journalism, which West contends is "untrue or misleading." Also, this legion of radicals merely is echoing accounts by most political scientists, their fellow leftists. Despite this criticism, too, West says "America always had had laws providing for the poor." I contend that while these laws have existed, from the federal level down to the smallest public entity, they constantly have been subverted by greedy, self-serving politicians, bureaucrats and union "goons." And most, but not all, have been Democrats immersed in municipal, county, state or federal regional make-work "machines" that I earlier described as nothing more than money-laundering operations administered largely by public-employee unions.

The Declaration of Independence contains a clear obligation to help the poor, and the Founders' policies "were intended to help the poor in ways that did not violate the rights of taxpayers or promote irresponsible behavior," West offers. Until 1965, there was a three-pronged recipe for success of any individual willing to adhere to the original precepts: 1. Free markets to protect property rights; 2. Provision of government support for lifelong marriage and general morality; and 3. Any poverty program was a last resort, with a minimal safety net for what Ronald Reagan later referred to as "the truly needy." West argues, quite lucidly, that, post-1965, there began definite tie-ins to concurrent breakdowns in morality and traditional relationships. (The year 1965 is interesting, too, in that the grandfather of the female student described at length in Chapter 7 graduated from high school in that year; he told me he was glad to graduate *exactly* in June 1965 because his California high school district introduced sex education classes the following fall.)

One of my favorite topic areas – and one on which I have developed a considerable amount of expertise and earned a certain status over the years – is that of illegal immigration and its relationship to national security. As the grandson of immigrants, I have always been fascinated by the legal processes our prescient forefathers placed in our Constitution, and how it is subverted on a daily basis by those who enter the United States illegally. As conservative icon Rush Limbaugh often reminds us, "What don't people understand about 'illegal'? I mean, the first act of these people upon entering our country is breaking the law." Here is what West writes:

> "America has a long and generous tradition of welcoming as equal citizens a larger number of immigrants, from a greater variety of national and religious origins, than any other nation in history. Shortly before the Civil War, Abraham Lincoln gave a beautiful speech in Chicago on the tie that binds American citizens together and makes them one people. There are many Americans, he said, who are not blood descendants of the American Founders. . . . Although Lincoln was speaking to European-Americans, there is nothing in his account of citizenship that is limited to Europeans. Any human being is capable of becoming an American, because the equality principle that defines American, as Lincoln wrote on another occasion, is 'an abstract truth, applicable to all men and all times'."

While until 1965, it was easier for Europeans to immigrate here legally, "the 1965 Immigration Act . . . in effect, made it harder for Europeans and easier for non-Europeans to come to America," West states. Carrying that thought further, I think this aspect has been greatly distorted in the opposite direction, and West agrees. "The prevailing view among mainstream scholars and in the popular media is that if we believe in human equality, it is unfair to deny entry to anyone." With this reasoning, there should be no borders and, therefore, absolutely no need for national security. This line of thinking is patently absurd, and dangerous to our safety and security to boot. West opines thusly:

> "The Founders supported the view that a nation may, and sometimes must, set limits on immigration, even to the point of considering national origin. But they based this view on the equality principle, not on its rejection."

Very similar views of immigration, West states, were largely held by the Founders, especially Washington, Hamilton and Jefferson, in that "first, America should generously welcome as equal citizens people from many nations and religions; second, the numbers and kinds of immigrants may need to be limited with a view to qualities of character required for democratic citizenship."

West discusses both the right and duty to exclude, both of which were implied in what was previously described as the equality principle and announced by the Founders in the Declaration of Independence and in several early state constitutions. He elaborates:

> "Just because the equality principle permits a people to decide which outsiders should be

admitted and which excluded, should this
right be exercised? If so, when and how?
(The Declaration) states the principles of just
government based on the equality principle.
First, the purpose of government is to secure
the citizens' equal rights to life, liberty, and
the pursuit of happiness. Second, government
must derive its just powers from the consent
of the governed. These two principles were
repeated over and over again in the founding
era. All of the leading American Founders
believed them to be true."

West ultimately concludes "that every people has a
right to exclude aliens that it deems undesirable, and a
duty to exclude aliens whose excessive numbers or
questionable character might endanger the citizens'
liberty."

Further, I agree completely with him that there are
various moral conditions of citizenship in a nation of laws
like ours, paramount of which is the role of public
education in maintaining freedom and promoting (but not
demeaning) morals, along with the promotion of various
commonly accepted general moral strictures, and self-
restraint and self-assertion among both government and
citizens. I would further add that there are two distinct
kinds of aliens: legal and illegal. And, as I have made
crystal-clear for a long time in taking the lead on this vital
national-security issue, there is no place in our country –
for *any* reason – for illegal aliens (regardless of any

sanitized description of them by The Associated Press or any other enabling left-wingers.)

Betsy McCaughey, the former lieutenant governor of New York, an acknowledged conservative expert on health-care issues and a steadfast opponent of Obamacare, writes that such reckless spending on illegal non-citizens pits elderly American citizens against illegals in a battle for diminishing resources. McCaughey reasons that "death panels" encased in the two thousand-plus pages of the Obama proposal (part or all of which will remain law unless repealed by Congress despite a March 2012 U.S. Supreme Court decision) provide a false choice by repealing beefed-up Medicare, then siphoning the funds into an expansion of Medicaid, including interpreter services for illegal aliens. "That's amazing," McCaughey states, "considering the wave of baby boomers entering Medicare in this decade," let alone already existing seniors. "There are ways to reduce federal health spending without cutting short grandma's life," especially when it additionally means kowtowing to the millions who already have illegally compromised our security by breaching our borders.

As I wrote this, the Obama administration was working feverishly to increase the number of immigrants in the United States, even in times of deep recession, in order to ensure a large pool of voters who will vote for more entitlements to exist and grow long after Obama leaves office. He is also intent upon dramatically increasing the number of Islamic immigrants in our country. In a new report, the Center for Immigration

Studies, an independent research institute that examines the impact of immigration on the United States, forecasts such a disturbing upswing. Among key findings:

-- In just a single year, 2010, our country admitted more than 300,000 visitors and immigrants from 16 selected countries. These individuals were admitted as non-immigrant visitors, refugees, asylees or permanent residents.

-- Nearly 58,000 of these were admitted as permanent residents. The vast majority of permanent admissions from high-risk countries were based on marriage to a U.S. citizen or as a refugee or asylee. Both of these categories are notorious for high fraud rates.

-- Over the last decade, well over 2.5 million people were admitted from these high-risk countries, with the largest numbers from Pakistan, Saudi Arabia, Lebanon and Iran. These numbers have been trending up over the past decade.

--These numbers suggest a disturbing shift away from the mindset that a more restrictive

admissions policy and consistently robust immigration law enforcement are necessary components of national security.

TOM TANCREDO

West's bottom line is that "the Founders aimed to form a body of citizens who would be capable of governing themselves *democratically* through elected representatives, while also governing themselves *reasonably* through policies that secured their own rights while respecting those of others." In other words, West is saying, government's job is to provide consent and protection, not to coddle illegal entrants to a sovereign nation.

From my viewpoint – which is shared by most other genuine immigration "purists" – our country can return to its customary lofty position of respect by truly securing our borders and showing better reciprocal attention to *legál* immigrants who honor our process. When we finally accomplish this, we also will be reversing the odious trampling of the Left on our cherished institutions.

Therefore, my own bottom line is this: In the spirit of vindicating the Founders, government exists to protect the common well-being by providing national defense, national security and protection only in a responsive, rather than pre-emptive, sense. That is the essence of what is referred to as "Peace Through Strength," or the country's readiness to protect – preparing and possessing security resources instead of having to gather them at the last minute when a necessary crisis calls for them. This all is supplemental to a "well-armed citizenry," as laid out in the Second Amendment to the U.S. Constitution. There is no moral or legal standing whatsoever for government to supplant any private institution with unnecessary, unwanted or undue regulations. If we, as Americans, do not focus on national defense and security, we lose our cherished freedoms – to the younger generation, this would mean no more Starbucks, no more Facebook, or no more ability to freely practice the religion of our choice.

EPILOGUE: MEMORY ROCK

As he roamed the Holy Land spreading the Word more than 2,000 years ago, Jesus Christ laid his gentle hand on the strong shoulder of the Apostle Peter and proclaimed unhesitatingly: "Now I say to you that you are Peter (which means 'rock'), and upon this rock I will build my church, and all the powers of hell will not conquer it." (*Matthew 16:18*)

Then, more than 1,600 years later, the Pilgrims, escaping religious persecution, sailed from England and landed at Plymouth Rock in what is present-day Massachusetts.

In either instance, the principals involved had been subject to the slings and arrows of sectarian intolerance. While many centuries have passed, the radical, anti-God environment has grown – to the point whereby what used to be considered lewd, immoral and unacceptable is the accepted norm, while any overt display of religion, no matter how subtle, is the equivalent of a criminal activity. This is all backwards, and it is a realization of "all the powers of hell" having arrived in a modern-day incarnation; they must not be allowed a permanent conquest over what is good and decent.

As a society in general, we need to revive the concept of a Memory Rock, not unlike the figurative boulder on which Jesus chose to build his church, or the literal natural foundation where the ship *Mayflower* dropped anchor. The firm rock on which to base our bearings must include eradicating rampant political correctness, reintroducing in our classrooms the teaching of the Three R's and allowing school prayer, outlawing racial and gender preferences, returning common sense to the nation's judicial benches, canceling onerous and unnecessary environmental regulations, reinstituting domestic drilling and mining for all primary forms of energy, stopping unnecessary and uncontrolled spending and, perhaps most important, securing our borders. We arrived at the current juncture by failing to maintain our moral standing; conscience has to be the primary counter-weight to anti-social behavior. This is one "rock" the Founders left us that we have totally ignored; we must get rid of our collective "amnesia" and remember the basis of our nation of laws and morality.

You have to agree with me and millions of others that America is connected to a place that can be definable, and that Western Civilization has real value. The concept of a nation of laws is clearly a Western value, not that of radicals whose basis for existence is at least a European socialist, if not outright Marxist, model.

Here is what I said about our culture in a speech on the U.S. House floor on May 5, 2003; it is exactly how I felt then, how I still feel, and it precisely sums up the daily danger that radicalism couched as false diversity presents to all of us:

"I believe that manufactured diversity in every facet of our life has a political motivation. It has nothing to do with toleration of other cultures. [...] I am gravely concerned that our current immigration is not of the same character of our historic immigration in that the impact and effect will be to weaken our civic culture and our political institutions that guarantee life, liberty and the pursuit of happiness. "

It has been said many times during presidential campaigns over the past two decades that "it's the economy, stupid!" While that is largely true when one sees how economics are mishandled and misunderstood by those at all levels of governmental power, there is something important that gets ignored: the cultural direction in which society continues to spiral dangerously downward. Therefore, the axiom should really be "it's the culture, stupid!" since societal issues at their base are morally more important than even the economy.

While the Culture War continues to become more pronounced, the nation grows more divided along cultural lines. This battle for the soul of our nation has metastasized over the last 50 years or less in terms of how we look at ourselves.

Being a truly "united" nation means commonality in values, language, goals, borders and religion (that is, from a Judeo/Christian basis). There used to be true assimilation whereby (legal) immigrants gave up past allegiances and severed ties to their old country (in a sense), creating the whole concept of American Exceptionalism – in other words, legitimately shared ideas rather than separate ideas that divide.

So-called progressives, over time, have been able to destroy everything we hold sacred by continuing to tear down our long-held and cherished collective values. It is all part of a cultural war, especially about whom we supposedly offend.

The phenomenon of political correctness is rampant in other countries as well. It has been my experience that people surrender liberty for security, as evidenced by the "I'll take care of you" attitude that fueled Barack Obama's 2012 re-election. Other recent examples are New York Mayor Michael Bloomberg's outlawing larger-size soft drinks and a New Jersey requirement to put dogs in car seats.

There is an immense battle occurring now that is ongoing, and "evil forces" are winning that battle – at least at present, unfortunately. Our end goal is to reverse all this radical ratcheting by grasping firmly onto the Memory Rock.

If the Great Experiment of 1776 fails, the lights go out all over the world.

SOURCE NOTES

A People's History of the United States: 1492-Present, Zinn, Howard. *Harper Perennial Modern Classics*, 2005

Revisionists.com (website), 2011

"Obama Revises His Record" (op-ed column), Limbaugh, David. *WorldNetDaily*, May 13, 2011

"Memory Rock". *Fort Worth Star-Telegram*, May 6, 2011

"Noam Chomsky Shamefully Defends bin Laden" (op-ed column), Dershowitz, Alan. *Newsmax.com*, May 11, 2011

"Would You Rather Obama Have Died Than bin Laden?" (Transcript of Television Interview of Tom Tancredo by Martin Bashir). *MSNBC*, May 11, 2011

Debate on U.S. Immigration: Former U.S. Rep. Tom Tancredo and Kris Kobach, Arizona Immigration Law Co-Author, vs. Tamar Jacoby of ImmigrationWorks USA and Mayor Julian Castro of San Antonio,Texas (transcript). *Bloomberg TV*, May 11, 2011

Noam Chomsky: Power and Terror: Post 9/11 Talks and Interviews, Junkerman, John and Masakazu, Takei, Editors. *Seven Stories Press, New York; Little More, Tokyo, 2003*

What If?: The World's Foremost Military Historians Imaging What Might Have Been, Essays by Stephen C. Ambrose, John Keenan, David McCullough, James M. McPherson and others; Robert Cowley, Editor. *G.P. Putnam Sons, 1999*

The American Heritage New History of the Civil War, Narrative by Bruce Catton; McPherson, James M., Editor and Introduction. *Viking, 1996*

The Souls of Black Folk, Du Bois, W.E.B. *Penguin Books, 1989*

Imperial Ambitions, Chomsky, Noam. *Metropolitan Books, Henry Holt & Co., New York, 2005*

9-11, Chomsky, Noam. *Seven Stories Press/New York, 2002*

Hopes and Prospects, Chomsky, Noam. *Haymarket Books, Chicago, Illinois,2010*

The New Military Humanism: Lessons from Kosovo, Chomsky, Noam. *Common Courage Press, Monroe, ME, 1999*

The Day Man Lost: Hiroshima, 6 August 1945, the Public War Research Society. *Kodansha International Ltd., 1972*

America's Hidden History, Davis, Kenneth C. *Smithsonian Books, Harper Collins,2008*

Marching Toward Freedom: Blacks in the Civil War, 1861-1865, McPherson, James M.; Scott, John Anthony, General Editor. *Alfred A. Knopf, Inc., 1967; Facts on File, New York, Oxford, 1965, 1967 and 1991*

Deterring Democracy, Chomsky, Noam. *Fall and Wag, a Division of Farrar, Straus and Giroux, New York, 1992*

Almost History, Bruns, Roger, *Hyperion, 2000*

The Civil War: Opposing Viewpoints, Leone, Bruno, Executive Editor; Bender, David L., Publisher. *Greenhaven Press, 1995*

Renegade for Peace and Justice, Congresswoman Lee, Barbara. *Bowman & Littlefield Publishers, Inc.,2008*

What They Fought For: 1861-1865, McPherson, James M. *Louisiana State University Press,1995*

A Power Government Cannot Suppress, Zinn, Howard. *City LightsBooks, 2007*

This Mighty Scourge: Perspectives on the Civil War, McPherson, James M. *Oxford University Press, 2007*

Declarations of Independence: Cross-Examining American Ideology, Zinn, Howard. *Harper Perennial, 1990*

Justice in Everyday Life: The Way It Really Works, Zinn, Howard. *South End Press, 1974 and 2002*

Vietnam: The Logic of Withdrawal, Zinn, Howard. *South End Press, 1967 and 2002*

Voices of a People's History of the United States, Zinn, Howard, and Arnove, Anthony. *Seven Stories Press, 2004*

The Unraveling Bush Presidency, Zinn, Howard. *Seven Stories Press, 2007*

The New American Crisis, Ruggiero, Greg, and Sahulka, Scott, editors. *The New Press, 1995*

Past Imperfect: History According to the Movies. *Henry Holt & Company, 1995*

The Abolitionist Legacy: from Reconstruction to the NAACP,McPherson, James M., Princeton University Press, 1975

"Yet Another Chapter in the Ward Churchill Saga" (editorial), *The Denver Post, June 2, 2011*

Oliver Stone Interviews, Edited by Charles L.P. Silet, *University Press Of Mississippi, 2001*

The Films of Oliver Stone, Edited by Don Kunz, *Scarecrow Press Inc., 1997*

Straight Talk from the Heartland, Schultz, Ed, *Regan Books, 2004*

Killer Politics, Schultz, Ed, *Hyperion, 2010*

Free Markets and Social Justice, Sunstein, Cass R., *Oxford University Press, 1997*

The Cost of Rights: Why Liberty Depends on Taxes, Holmes, Stephen, and Sunstein, Cass R., *W.W. Norton and Company, 1999*

One Case at a Time: Judicial Minimalism on the Supreme Court, Sunstein, Cass R., *Harvard University Press, 1999*

The Second Bill of Rights, Sunstein, Cass R., *Basic Books, 2004*

On Rumors, Sunstein, Cass R., *Farrar, Straus and Giroux, 2009*

Fugitive Days (a memoir), Ayers, Bill, *Beacon Press, 2001*

Do the Media Govern, Iyengar, Shanto, and Reeves, Richard, Editors, *SAGE Publications, 1997*

"Liberalism: Life with Ann Curry" (op-ed column), Bozell, Brent, *GOPUSA.com; Creators.com, June 15, 2011*

"Students Stumble Again on the Basics of History" (news story), Banchero, Stephanie, *WSJ.com, June 14, 2011*

"Blacks' Role in Confederacy Remains Touchy Subject" (feature story),
Elder, Renee, *Associated Press;Yahoo.com, June 14, 2011*
"Just How Far Has America Fallen?" (website commentary), Eberle,
Bobby, *The Loft, GOPUSA.com;* excerpted from *AZCentral.com, June 17,2011*
"Jamie Oliver's Crusade Leads to Ban on Flavored Milk" (commentary),
RelaxNews, *Independent.co.uk, June 18, 2011*
"Tucson's Rejected Ethnic Studies Praised by Audit" (news account),
Associated Press; KTAR.com, June 18, 2011
"Don't Know Much About History" (interview with David McCullough),
Bolduc, Brian, *WSJ.com, June 19, 2011*
Agenda: Grinding America Down (documentary film), Bowers, Curtis,
Producer, Director and Writer, June 2011
"Don't Know Much About History" (op-ed column), Jacoby, Jeff,
Boston Globe, June 19, 2011
"The Deep Shame of Vancouver" (op-ed column), Warren, David,
Ottawa Citizen, June 19, 2011
"Arizona Schools Look at Florida As Successful Reform Model"
(news analysis), Kossan, Pat, *Arizona Republic; AZCentral.com, June 19, 2011*

"Why I Turned My Back on Liberalism" (interview with David Mamet), Gould, Martin, and Collie, Tim, *Newsmax.com, June 19, 2011*

Cambium Learning Group (website), *June 2011*

Abstract, State Board of Education and Textbook Committee, Mallan,Cheryl, University of Texas, Brownsville, EDCI 6334, Summer 2010

"The Dumbing-Down of America" (op-ed column), Buchanan, Pat, *Yahoo.com; Creators.com, June 21. 2011*

Wikipedia, Biographical entry on Jay Bennish, *Wikimedia Foundation,Inc., last modified, March 10, 2011*

"Bachmann: Queen of the Tea Party" (profile), Continetti, Matthew, *The Weekly Standard; RealClearPolitics.com, June 25, 2011*

Vindicating the Founders, West, Thomas G., *Rowmann & Littlefield Publishers, 1997*

"Constitution Still Matters to Some" (op-ed column), Rosen, Mike, *Denver Post, July 7, 2011*

"Casey Anthony: Single Mom of the Year" (op-ed column), Coulter, Ann, *WND.com, July 7, 2011*

"He's Baack! Vann Jones Getting Cozy with Pelosi, House Dems" (commentary), Klein, Aaron, *WND.com ,July 7, 2011*

"Tea Party Groups: Socialist UN Effort Trickles Down to U.S. Local Government" (news report), *Newsmax.com, July 7, 2011*

"Did White House Approve Project Gunrunner?" (op-ed column), Tancredo, Tom, *WND.com, June 18, 2011*

"California Lawmakers Order Gay History Included in Textbooks" (news report), N*ewsmax.com/Bloomberg News, July 5, 2011*

"Harvard: July 4th Is a GOP Holiday" (news report), *Newsmax.com, July 3, 2011*

"Look Who's Launching Anti-Tea Party Group" (commentary), Klein, Aaron, *WND.com, June 28, 2011*

"Feds Find Fix Was In on 'Study' of Homosexuality in Ranks" (news report), *WND.com, June 28, 2011*

"Gross Media Ignorance About the Founders" (op-ed column), Williams, Walter, *RealClearPolitics, July 5, 2011*

"History Books Get Gay Makeover" (op-ed column), Reagan, Michael, *Newsmax.com, July 9, 2011*

"OPS Buys 8,000 Diversity Manuals" (news report), Dejka, Joe, *Omaha World-Herald, July 12, 2011*

"Government Schools As Propaganda Mills" (op-ed column), Patton, Doug, *GOPUSA.com, July 13, 2011*

W.E.B. Du Bois: An Autobiography, Horne, Gerald, *Greenwood Press, 2010*

"Colorado Child Care Rules Could Require Racially Diverse Dolls,'Culturally Sensitive' Activities," *Denver Post, July 25, 2011*

The Secret Knowledge: On the Dismantling of American Culture, Mamet, David, *Sentinel,2011*

"American Psychological Association Supports Same-Sex 'Marriage' 157-0, *LifeSiteNews.com, August 8, 2011*

Dreams from My Father, Obama, Barack, *Three Rivers Press, 1995, 2004*

The Audacity of Hope, Obama, Barack, *Crown Publishers, 2006*

"ACORN Behind Occupy Wall Street Protest" (op-ed column), *JudicialWatch.org, Oct. 7, 2011*

"Tom Tancredo: Obama Elected Because 'We Do Not Have A Civics, Literacy Test' To Vote (report), *Huffington Post, July 15, 2011*

"Beheading of Children, Hangings Will Make People 'Fall in Line' ", *Occupy Wall Street website, Oct.15, 2011*

"Gross Media Ignorance About the Founders" (op-ed column), Walter Williams, *RealClearPolitics.com, July 5, 2011*

"Islamist Join Occupy Wall Street Protests," (news report), *Newsmax.com, Oct. 24,2011*

"Insanity: Jesse Jackson Calls on Government to Hire All Unemployed Americans for $40,000 Each," (news report),*U.S. Constitutional Press/Word Press, Oct.15,2011*

"Radical Children's Literature Being Distributed at OWS Protests," (news report), *U.S.Constitutional Press/Word Press, Oct.18, 2011*

"Seattle Fleabagger accused of exposing self to children," (news report), *U.S.Constitutional Press/Word Press, Oct.18,2011*

"Democrats Rent a Mob to "Occupy Wall Street'," (op-ed column), Malkin, Michelle, *Newsletter,TeaParty.org, Oct. 17, 2011*

"Nazis and Communists Throw Their Support Behind Occupy Wall Street (fleabagger) Movements," (news report), *U.S.Constitutional Press/Word Press, Oct.16, 2011*

"Proof! Wall Street protests no 'spontaneous uprising'," (op-ed column), Klein, Aaron, *WorldNetDaily, Oct.6, 2011*

"Protest mob is enjoying rich diet," (news report), Rosenberg, Rebecca, *NewYork Post, Oct. 20, 2011*

"The 'Occupiers don not represent Americans or their beliefs'," (editorial), *Washington Examiner,Oct.16, 2011*

"Don't Give Us Your Tired, Your Poor, Your Huddled Masses" Says Intelligence Squared US Immigration Debate Audience," (debate transcript), *National Public Radio,Bloomberg TV, May 9, 2011*

"Occupy Wall Street's Anti-Semitism Condemned," (news report), *Newsmax.com, Oct. 18, 2011*

"Occupy Wall Street: A Manifesto for {insert date}," (op-ed column), Hinkle, Barton, *RealClearPolitics.com, Oct. 18, 2011*

"The Deep Shame of Vancouver," (op-ed column), Warren, David, *Ottawa Citizen, RealClearPolitics.com, June 19, 2011*

"Healthcare Spending Pits Elderly Against Illegal Aliens," (op-ed column), McCaughey, Betsy, *Newsmax.com, Oct. 31, 2011*

"Uncle Sam Is No Venture Capitalist," (editorial), *Morning Bell, The Heritage Foundation, Oct. 3, 2011*

"Occupy the Future," (op-ed column), Chomsky, Noam, *In These Times, RealClearPolitics.com, Nov. 3, 2011*

Rush Limbaugh Show (radio transcript vignette), *Nov. 3,2011*

9Want to Know(TV debate video), *KUSA-TV, Nov.2, 2011*

"My Comments on Occupy Oakland," (web posting), Rep. Lee, Barbara, *Huffington Post, Nov. 6, 2011*

List of Obama Administration "Czars," (website), *FoxNews.com,Nov. 5, 2011*

"Obama delays oil pipeline from Canada despite job starved economy," (news story), Daly, Matthew, *Associated Press, GOPUSA.com, Nov. 12,2011*

"Obama's Keystone Evasion," (blog opinion), Hinderaker, John, *Power Line, RealClearPolitics.com, Nov. 12, 2011*

"Smithsonian 'Sent Representatives' to Collect 'Occupy' Memorabilia to 'Document Spirit of American Democracy," Zellers, Lucas, *CNSNews.com, Nov. 13, 2011*

"GQ Thinks Ed Schultz is one of "The Least Influential People Alive," Ariens, Chris, *MediaBistro.com/TV Newser/GQ, Nov. 25, 2011*

"Memo to Gingrich: 'Red Card' is path to amnesty," (op-ed column), Tancredo, Tom, *WorldNetDaily.com, Nov. 26, 2011*

"How the EPA May Cost You Thousands," (editorial), *Morning Bell,The Heritage Foundation, Nov. 29, 2011*

"How Much Will Proposed EPA Regulations Cost Us?" (editorial), *AskHeritage.org*, Dec. 2, 2011

"Agenda 21 and the Threat in Your Backyard," (editorial), *Morning Bell, The Heritage Foundation, Dec. 5, 2011*

"California's Not Dreamin': This Is the Nightmare of an Obama Second Term," (op-ed column), Hedgecock, Roger, *Human Events.com, Dec. 9, 2011*

The Naked Communist, Skousen, W. Cleon, *Ensign Publishing Co.,1958*

"Fewer Americans See U.S. Divided Into 'Haves,' 'Have Nots', *Gallup Poll,Gallup.com,Dec. 27, 2011*

"Public Schools Teach the ABCs of Islam," Stakelbeck, Eric, *for CBN News, Oct. 9, 2008*

"U.S. Textbooks: Muslims Discovered America," *Patriot Update, January 2012*

"Taking Aim at CPAC," Tancredo, Tom, *American Patrol Report, Feb.11, 2012*

The Amazing Grace of Freedom: The Inspiring Faith of William Wilberforce, the Slaves' Champion, Baehr , Ted; Wales, Susan; Wales, Ken, *New Leaf Press, 2007*

William Wilberforce: The Life of the Great Anti-Slave Trade Campaigner, Hague, William, *Harcourt, 2007*

"Education or Indoctrination? The Treatment of Islam in 6th through12th Grade American Textbooks," *ACT! for America Education, March 2012*

Ameritopia, Levin, Mark R., *Threshold Editions, 2012*

Barack Obama and the Enemies Within, Loudon, Trevor, *2011*

"The Trayvon Martin the Media Is Hiding, Tancredo, Tom, *tomtancredo.com, March 26, 2012*

"After Only 29 Months of Obama, Here's Your Change Obama Promised You!", *The Heritage Foundation, U.S. Bureau of Labor Statistics, U.S. Energy Information Administration, U.S. Census Bureau, U.S. Departmentof Labor, U.S. Department of Agriculture, Wall Street Journal, The ConferenceBoard, U.S. Department of Treasury, Federal Reserve, Federal Housing and Finance Administration, Federal Deposit Insurance Corp., Standard & Poor's/Case-Shiller.*

"Multiple Suspensions Paint Complicated Portrait of Trayvon Martin,"Robles, Frances, *The Miami Herald, March 26, 2012*

"Weekend of Violence Claims 10 Shooting Victims Across Chicago,"Ford, Liam; Nickeas, Peter; and Sobol, Rosemary, *Chicago Tribune, March 26,2012*

"A Youth 'OnTrack' Until Fatal Gunfire," Esquivel, Paloma; Pringle,Paul; and Vara-Orta, Francisco, *Los Angeles Times, March 4, 2008*

"Lynching George Zimmerman – Overwhelming America's Historic White Majority," Bradley, Peter, *V DARE.com, March 25, 2012*

"Vast Inflows of Middle East Immigrants, Visitors May Put U.S. at Risk," *Center for Immigration Studies, March 27, 2012*

"Piven Uses Class Lecture to Lay Out Strategy to Illegally Occupy Foreclosed Homes, Default on Student Debt," Johnson, Benny, *TheBlazecom, May 12, 2012*

"Obama's Desperate Amnesty Gamble," Tancredo, Tom, *WND, June 23,2012*

"Who Shall Defend the Constitution?", Tancredo, Tom, *WND, June 30, 2012*

"Cowardly Republicans: Impeach Obama Now," Tancredo, Tom, *WND, July 28, 2012*

"America's Future: No Longer Worth Celebrating," Tancredo,Tom, *WND, July 20,2012*

"Impeach Obama for Treason," Tancredo, Tom, *WND, Nov. 3, 2012*

"Identity Politics Triumph," Tancredo, Tom, *WND, Nov. 10, 2012*

"Time to Retool and Reload," Tancredo, Tom, *WND, Nov. 17, 2012*

"Sen. Tim Scott: 'Not Black Enough'," Tancredo, Tom, *WND, Jan. 5, 2013*

"Senate Amnesty: Non-Enforcement Is Chief Goal," Tancredo, Tom, *WND, May 11, 2013*

"3 Reasons Benghazi Still Matters," *Western Center for Journalism, May 12, 2013*

HATING AMERICA

<u>ACKNOWLEDGMENTS</u>

There always are far too many people to thank by name when a book is put together, but we want to single out a select few – for various reasons.

From a support and feedback standpoint, there are the likes of Nancy McKiernan, Barbara Kralis, Chuck Swift and Rob Roseman, to name just a few.

Then a special nod goes to the patient, knowledgeable staff at Amazon and Kindle Direct Publishing, true 21st-century resources for any author.

But mostly, if Jackie Tancredo and Maria Ross weren't around with the rest of our loving families to keep us on an even keel, we couldn't function as contributing members of society who are willing to take the slings and arrows projected our way for adhering to our time-tested beliefs.

Finally, praise the Good Lord for giving us the requisite gifts that allow us to do whatever it is that we do.

TOM TANCREDO and PHIL ROSS

TOM TANCREDO

ABOUT THE AUTHORS

Tom Tancredo served a decade in the U.S. House of Representatives, being elected and routinely re-elected by voters in the Sixth Congressional District in the Denver, Colo., suburbs. Prior to that he was a school teacher, elected to three terms in the Colorado House of Representatives, regional director for the U.S. Department of Education, and president of the Independence Institute, a free-market think tank. Since leaving Congress in 2009, he has founded and heads the Rocky Mountain Foundation, and is founder of The American Legacy Alliance. Tancredo also was an early entrant competing for the 2008 GOP presidential nomination and the candidate of the American Constitution Party in the 2010 Colorado governor's race. He has hosted a weeknight talk show on KVOR-AM in Colorado Springs. He is a graduate of the University of Northern Colorado. Tancredo's first book, *In Mortal Danger*, published in 2005, details the dire state of our porous borders and laxity in national security. A native of Colorado, he lives with his wife in the Denver area.

Phil Ross has more than 30 years' award-winning experience as a sportswriter, news editor and reporter, and editorial page editor on daily newspapers and in public relations. He has worked on daily newspapers in California, Nevada, Texas and Colorado, including *The Anaheim Bulletin, Orange Coast Daily Pilot, Ventura County Star-Free Press, Daily Commercial News, Las Vegas Review-Journal, El Paso Times* and *Daily News-Press*. He is former majority communications officer for the Colorado House of Representatives. Ross earned a degree in Mass Communication from Cal State Hayward (now Cal State East Bay) and is an honorably discharged Vietnam Era veteran of the U.S. Army. In addition to covering everything from high school sports to pro football, he worked as a freelancer on the professional rodeo circuit, including covering the National Finals Rodeo. He also was a college and high school baseball umpire for 18 years. He lives with his wife in the Denver area.

HATING AMERICA

"Hating America: The Left's Long History of Despising (and Slowly Destroying) Our Great Country" uses the keen insights, often based on first-hand dealings with those who would tear down this country, of former five-term Congressman Tom Tancredo. From his perspective as a national and international leader on border and security issues, the former history teacher and former U.S. Department of Education official deconstructs faulty conclusions and false premises by the various shades of radicals in each succeeding chapter. Tancredo, bolstered by the expertise and research of former longtime journalist, public relations practitioner and political "junkie" Phil Ross, sets the stage of attack by debunking the fallacious theories, piece by piece. Fueled by incredible minutiae about the most notorious anti-American critics, both current and from throughout history – who unbelievably consider themselves the ultimate patriots – the book makes a compelling case to debunk all of them. The fearless Tancredo, rarely a stranger to controversy when the truth is on the line, relates many never-before-published recollections and personal encounters. Included are some of his most-notable moments in face-to-face debates and confrontations with left-wing radicals of all stripes. Along the way, Tancredo not only deconstructs the anti-patriots, but offers viable solutions to counter them. The book is designed to illustrate how America is being literally destroyed to the core of its collective soul, as these reckless, dangerous radicals gradually but forcefully continue to gain a foothold on the American *psyche*. "Hating America" emerges as an extremely timely read, helping clarify why this radicalism must be stopped in its tracks as soon as possible. It is important that, to better grasp what is happening to our republic, the public must understand the historical pattern of how the Left always has despised this country by slowly destroying it.

Made in the USA
Middletown, DE
07 May 2023

30207060R00159